THE OCTOROON

Photographer unknown, *Dion Boucicault*, 1878.

THE OCTOROON

Dion Boucicault

a *Broadview Anthology of British Literature* edition

Contributing Editor, *The Octoroon*:
Sarika Bose, University of British Columbia

General Editors,
Broadview Anthology of British Literature:
Joseph Black, University of Massachusetts, Amherst
Leonard Conolly, Trent University
Kate Flint, University of Southern California
Isobel Grundy, University of Alberta
Don LePan, Broadview Press
Roy Liuzza, University of Tennessee
Jerome J. McGann, University of Virginia
Anne Lake Prescott, Barnard College
Barry V. Qualls, Rutgers University
Claire Waters, University of California, Davis

broadview press

Library and Archives Canada Cataloguing in Publication

Boucicault, Dion, 1820-1890, author
        The octoroon / Dion Boucicault ; contributing editor, The
Octoroon: Sarika Bose, University of British Columbia ; general
editors, Broadview anthology of British literature: Joseph Black,
University of Massachusetts, Amherst, Leonard Conolly, Trent
University, Kate Flint, University of Southern California, Isobel
Grundy, University of Alberta, Don LePan, Broadview Press, Roy
Liuzza, University of Tennessee, Jerome J. McGann, University of
Virginia, Anne Lake Prescott, Barnard College, Barry V. Qualls,
Rutgers University, Claire Waters, University of California, Davis.

(A Broadview anthology of British literature edition)
Includes bibliographical references.
ISBN 978-1-55481-211-0 (pbk.)

        1. Slavery—Louisiana—Drama. 2. Slaves—Louisiana—Drama.
3. Plantations—Louisiana—Drama. 4. Racially mixed women—
Louisiana—Drama. 5. Love—Drama. 6. Louisiana—Drama. I. Title.
II. Series: Broadview anthology of British literature

PR4161.B2O3 2014   822'.8   C2014-902422-3

Broadview Press is an independent, international publishing house, incorporated in 1985.

We welcome comments and suggestions regarding any aspect of our publications—please feel free to contact us at the addresses below or at broadview@broadviewpress.com.

North America	PO Box 1243, Peterborough, Ontario K9J 7H5, Canada
	555 Riverwalk Parkway, Tonawanda, NY 14150, USA
	Tel: (705) 743-8990; Fax: (705) 743-8353
	email: customerservice@broadviewpress.com
UK, Europe, Central Asia,	Eurospan Group, 3 Henrietta St., London WC2E 8LU, UK
Middle East, Africa, India,	Tel: 44 (0) 1767 604972; Fax: 44 (0) 1767 601640
and Southeast Asia	email: eurospan@turpin-distribution.com
Australia and New Zealand	NewSouth Books, c/o TL Distribution
	15-23 Helles Ave., Moorebank, NSW 2170, Australia
	Tel: (02) 8778 9999; Fax: (02) 8778 9944
	email: orders@tldistribution.com.au

www.broadviewpress.com

Developmental Editors: Jennifer McCue and Laura Buzzard

Contributing Writer: Jude Polsky

Broadview Press acknowledges the financial support of the Government of Canada through the Canada Book Fund for our publishing activities.

PRINTED IN CANADA

Contents

Introduction • 7
  A Note on the Text • 19

The Octoroon; or, Life in Louisiana • 21

In Context • 77
  American Reviews • 77
    "'The Octoroon.' A Disgrace to the North, a Libel on the South,"
      Spirit of the Times; A Chronicle of the Turf, Agriculture, Field Sports,
      Literature and the Stage (17 December 1859) • 77
    from "The Octoroon" *The Charleston Courier, Tri-Weekly*
      (22 December 1859) • 83
    from "Winter Garden—First Night of 'The Octoroon,'" *The New*
      York Herald (7 December 1859) • 84
  English Reviews • 87
    "Saving the Octoroon," *Punch* (21 December 1861) • 87
    from "Theatres and Music," *John Bull* (Saturday, 23 November
      1861) • 89
    from "Adelphi" (Review of *The Octoroon*), *The Athenaeum*
      (23 November 1861) • 92
    "Pan at the Play," *Fun* (Saturday, 30 November 1861) • 94
    "Adelphi Theatre" (Review of Revised Play), *The Times* [London]
      (12 December 1861) • 94
    "Pan at the Play," *Fun* (Saturday, 21 December 1861) • 96
  Letters to Editors Concerning the Lawsuit • 97
    "The Octoroon Conflict: Financial and Political View of the Case—
      Letter from Mrs. Agnes Robertson Bourcicault," *The New York*
      Herald (Friday, 16 December 1859) • 97
  A Selection of Letters from Boucicault Defending the Content of *The*
    Octoroon • 99
    "Letter from the Author of the 'Octoroon,'" *The New York Herald*
      (7 December 1859) • 99
    "The Octoroon Gone Home," *New York Times* (9 February
      1860) • 100
    "'The Octoroon': To the Editor of the Times," *The Times* [London]
      (Wednesday, 20 November 1861) • 102

Boucicault on Acting • 104

   from Dion Boucicault, "The Art of Acting" (1882) • 104

Alternative Endings • 107

   The Illustrated London News (14 December 1861) • 107

   "Music and the Drama," *Bell's Life in London and Sporting Chronicle* (Sunday, 15 December 1861) • 107

   from *The Octoroon*: Founded on Dion Boucicault's Celebrated and Original Melodrama (1897) • 108

   from Dion Boucicault, *The Octoroon*, Lacy's Acting Edition, No. 963 (c.1861) • 108

   from Dion Boucicault, *The Octoroon: A Drama in Three Acts* (26 October 1861) • 116

On Slavery • 118

   from Dion Boucicault, unpublished note, Theatre Museum, London (1861) • 118

   from Fredrika Bremer, "Fredrika Bremer Sees the New Orleans Slave Market" (1853) • 119

   from *Civil Code of the State of Louisiana* (1825) • 122

Illustrations • 124

   from *The Illustrated London News* (30 November 1861) • 124

   Cover, *Reynolds Miscellany* (4 January 1862) • 125

   Cover, *The Octoroon* (Dick's Standard Plays) • 126

Permissions Acknowledgments • 127

Introduction

Dion Boucicault
1820–1890

Not many people today recognize the name Dion Boucicault (pronounced "Boo-see-coe") or know of his plays. They might, however, have some awareness of an iconic scene from one of the first silent films, *After Dark*, adapted from a Boucicault play, in which a woman is tied to a railroad track while an oncoming train rushes toward her. Regarded by Bernard Shaw as a master of the theater, Boucicault was arguably the most important figure in drama in North America and Britain during the second half of the nineteenth century, writing or adapting more than 130 plays (as well as producing and acting in many of them) and introducing numerous theatrical innovations. He was instrumental in establishing American copyright law; he is also thought to have been the first playwright to receive royalty payments, instead of a standard fee for writing; and he created the concept of the touring company (before his time producers would always hire new actors for productions in different cities). Although he was adept at discerning and writing for prevailing public tastes, his plays, many of which are melodramas, were eventually eased off the stage by realistic dramas, and they have not been widely revived in modern times.

Boucicault was born Dionysius Lardner Boursiquot in Dublin to Anna Maria Darley, who came from a literary family. His father's identity is uncertain, as he took his name from both Samuel Smith Boursiquot, Anna's much older husband, and Dionysius Lardner, her lover, who became the boy's guardian. At the age of eight, Boucicault and most of his siblings settled in London with their mother—Boursiquot joined them for a time and then returned to Dublin—and from then on his schooling was overseen by Lardner. He did not attend university, having determined early on that he would be an actor.

Boucicault's first success as a playwright came at the age of 21, when *London Assurance* (1841) was performed at Covent Garden by well-known actors and became an immediate hit. After subsequent plays performed to lukewarm audiences, Boucicault, who was deeply in debt, went to Paris in search of French plays that could be adapted for the British stage. It was there he met and married Anne Guiot, an older woman of means, who died just three years later under mysterious circumstances. Thus began a love life that was no less controversial than his mother's had been. His second marriage was to actress Agnes Robertson, the adopted daughter of Charles Kean, a famous Shakespearean actor and manager of the theater that produced many of Boucicault's plays. The couple had six children together. At the height of their popularity, Boucicault and Robertson moved to New York to cash in on the lucrative American theater market; they then spent several years in London and other British cities, where they experienced great popular success but also some serious financial mishaps, before eventually returning to New York. Later, when Boucicault was estranged from Robertson but still married to her, he married Louise Thorndyke, an actress 43 years his junior, while they were working on a production in Australia. Robertson responded with a very public outcry, and the American press and public alike condemned his immorality and insensitivity. When Boucicault and Thorndyke returned to the States, however, theatergoers went in droves to witness the scandalous couple perform on stage.

Never one to shy away from scandal, Boucicault often raised controversial subjects in his plays, albeit with a canny eye to popular taste. In *The Octoroon; or, Life in Louisiana*, first performed in 1859 in New York, he took a pro-abolitionist, anti-racist stance on slavery. When the play ran in Britain, Boucicault succumbed to the public's desire for a happy ending and rewrote the conclusion.

Boucicault's career was marked by a series of very successful runs, with some years seeing productions of more than six different plays. His Irish plays, in particular *The Colleen Bawn* (1860), *Arrah-na-Pogue* (1864), and *The Shaughraun* (1874), were extremely popular. *The Colleen Bawn* played on stage 230 times in its first London run—a record number of performances at that time—and was attended three times by Queen Victoria. Although successes like this earned Boucicault the moniker "the Irish Shakespeare," in his later years he was saddled by debt and saddened by his waning popularity; "I have written for a monster who forgets," he wrote. Boucicault died in New York in 1890. Only one of his children attended the funeral.

The Octoroon

[Warning: Some details regarding *The Octoroon*'s ending are discussed in this introduction to the play.]

Play Origins and Abolitionism in Literature

The American Civil War (1861–65) and the abolition of slavery had yet to take place when Dion Boucicault wrote *The Octoroon*, but during the 1840s and 1850s anti-slavery rhetoric became increasingly difficult to ignore in America. Activists, politicians, and writers of fiction launched many different sorts of campaigns to raise awareness of the evils of slavery. John Brown, hanged a few days before the New York opening of *The Octoroon*, carried out violent attacks against slave owners and aimed to incite widespread rebellion among slaves. Lydia Maria Francis Child wrote several abolitionist works, such as *An Appeal in Favor of That Class of Americans Called Africans* (1833), which strongly condemned slavery and the laws of miscegenation, and called for immediate abolition, with no compensation to be given to slave owners.

The inspiration for the play can be seen in many literary anti-slavery short stories such as Child's own "The Quadroons" (1842) or "Slavery's Pleasant Homes: A Faithful Sketch" (1843); poems such as Henry Wadsworth Longfellow's "The Quadroon Girl" (1842); and novels such as Harriet Beecher Stowe's *Uncle Tom's Cabin* (1852) or Thomas Mayne Reid's *The Quadroon: Or, A Lover's Adventures in Louisiana* (1856). For a writer of melodrama, a genre that specialized in tales of injustice imposed on the downtrodden, the subject of slavery was irresistible. Mayne Reid's novel appears to have been the immediate inspiration for Boucicault's play, but the figure of the "tragic mulatta" was commonplace in much anti-slavery literature. The plot trajectory, with little variation, tended to dismantle the initially secure socio-economic status of a seemingly white young woman on the basis of the revelation of her African heritage (Zoe is, as the play's title suggests, an "octoroon"—someone with one-eighth black ancestry). In a society that relied on genetic technicalities, misinformation, and the criminalization of ethnic difference to maintain its power structures and its identity, it was not possible for a mixed-race character to be reintegrated into her former community and recover her former status. In such a society it rang true that in the end there could be no alternative for Zoe other than a tragic one—a fact reflected in the ending written for the original version of the play, which first opened in New York.

The Play's Production

By the time *The Octoroon* opened at the Winter Garden Theatre in New York on 6 December 1859, Dion Boucicault was already a famous and commercially successful playwright on both sides of the Atlantic. *The Octoroon* was one of the most controversial plays of his career; it offended pro-slavery audiences who saw it as a condemnation of the institution of slavery, but it also offended anti-slavery audiences, who saw it as portraying slavery as a benevolent institution. According to Joseph Jefferson, the popular American comedian who played Scudder in New York, there were "various opinions as to which way the play leaned—whether it was Northern or Southern in its sympathy. The truth of the matter is, it was non-committal. The dialogue and the characters of the play made one feel for the South, but the action proclaimed against slavery and called loudly for its abolition." When the play opened in London on 18 November 1861, English audiences were equally offended by the tragic ending that had appealed to American audiences, who would not have accepted a marriage between the mixed blood title character and the Southern slave-owner.

Boucicault, a shrewd businessman, whetted the public's appetite for *The Octoroon* in advance by publicizing several behind-the-scenes dramas concerning its actors and its content. For example, his wife apparently received a death threat for planning to play a mixed-race character. Although in a letter to the *New York Times* he claimed to be surprised at the sensation caused by the play's anti-slavery stance, it is unlikely that his surprise was genuine, given his own experiences during his residence in New Orleans.

In the American production of *The Octoroon*, Boucicault himself played Wahnotee, the Native American character, which allowed the playwright an opportunity to display his skills as a physical actor; some reviewers disparagingly suggested that Wahnotee's inarticulateness in languages recognizable to the white characters and the English audience was appropriate for the acting skills of the author. Boucicault's wife, Agnes Robertson, played the title role of Zoe, the Octoroon. Although Robertson's portrayal of Zoe was unanimously praised by audiences in New York and London, some reviewers found it either inappropriate or unconvincing that the "Octoroon" should be played by a woman who looked so obviously Caucasian. Her gentle and civilized manners also offended some audience members by challenging assumptions about the intellectual and moral faculties of anyone with African blood. The popular American comedian Joseph Jefferson played the Yankee overseer, Salem Scudder, a role Boucicault took over when the play was produced in London.

The Octoroon created a sensation in New York; that Boucicault and his wife received $1,363 as their share of the first week's receipts gives some idea of the play's commercial success. However, within a week, Boucicault had disagreed violently with his business partner, William Stuart, and he and his wife walked out on the production to join the rival theater company of Laura Keene, the first woman producer in the States. The disagreement with Stuart led to a long-running lawsuit over copyright ownership, as Stuart simply replaced Boucicault and Robertson and continued the play's run without the playwright's permission. (It ran until 12 February 1860.)

The play's London premiere was as eagerly anticipated as its New York one, with several newspaper columnists discussing the coming production for months. Boucicault was if anything more famous in Britain than he was in America, and the play itself already had a lively history. Not everything went smoothly with the new production, however. There was a delay in the opening date, and a manuscript submitted to the Lord Chamberlain's Office for licensing reveals that Boucicault was making some changes in the order of scenes in the middle of the play and expanding on some of the exchanges between characters. At the beginning of Act 3, for example, an extra scene shows an exchange between Zoe and M'Closky after he has bought her.[1] (The scene also develops and underlines Zoe's independence of character and her refusal to compromise herself, even at the expense of remaining a slave when the alternative of living a comfortable life as M'Closky's mistress is offered to her.)

British reviewers expressed strong disapproval at the tragic ending of the play, criticizing it as an aesthetic even more than an ethical failure. Boucicault had disappointed the expectations of an audience educated in the conventions of the melodramatic genre, which, in the words of Oscar Wilde's Miss Prism, fulfilled the mission of fiction to let "the good end happily, the bad, unhappily." (It may be worth noting here that Zoe was played in the production by an actress known to be of "pure" Caucasian ethnicity; for the audience, that fact may have provided a degree of comfortable distance from the play's central dilemma.)

In response to this criticism, Boucicault revised the play's ending, with Zoe's reprieve and averted suicide first presented on 9 December 1861, and *The Octoroon* soon became an even greater sensation in London than in New York. Several songs and musical scores based on *The Octoroon* were published, "The Octoroon Galop" notable among them. In fact, *The Octoroon* became so fashionable that in the summer of 1862, a horse named "Octoroon" competed in all the major horse races, and a yacht named "Octoroon" raced in all the major regattas!

The Octoroon and Melodrama

Nineteenth-century melodramas aimed to touch the heart and to intensify emotional experience; their emotional high points were achieved through deliberately sensational scenes, often showing violent separations of family members or moments of seemingly insurmountable danger. Injustice was a central thematic concern for melodramatists, as it could be relied on to invoke strong emotional responses. The recognition and overcoming of injustice became the fundamental plot trajectory in many melodramas, which often addressed social problems predicated on an uneven distribution of political and economic power. Boucicault was a skilled and commer-

---

1   For more information, see *The Octoroon: A Drama in Three Acts* in the appendices.

cially minded melodramatist who knew how to use conventional plot devices with great effectiveness, and knew too how to employ highly emphatic and emotional language to signal moments of sincerity and drive home the moral and political thrust of the play. The defiant language Zoe uses in response to exhortations to accept her situation exemplifies the sort of political content often found in melodramas—as do George and Scudder's lectures to the plantation owners about decent behavior (whether in their attitudes towards race or towards vigilante justice).

By its nature melodrama relies on stock characters, and *The Octoroon* is no exception. Occupying central roles are the valiant Hero and romantic lover (George Peyton) who is ineffectual in practical terms, the Secondary Hero/Repentant Villain (Scudder) who is crucial to the resolution of the plot, the Heroine (Zoe) who is separated by circumstance and misunderstanding from the hero, and the First Villain (M'Closky) whose main role is to displace the hero and heroine from their legitimate places in society as well as to jeopardize the heroine's honor. The rest of the characters can be divided into groups that parallel the treatment accorded different social classes in the British melodramas so familiar to Boucicault. The plantation owners, wives, and daughters constitute the upper-class society of the play; slaves appear where peasants or working-class characters would have normally appeared on the London stage. Stock roles of the Comic Man (Pete), the innocent child targeted by the villain (Paul), and the Secondary Heroine rejected in love (Dora) are also powerfully present in *The Octoroon*.

A plot device that appears frequently in nineteenth-century melodramas and in the well-made plays is the emergence of a secret document—or, in the case of *The Octoroon*, multiple documents. The indolence and incompetence of Judge Peyton with his paperwork places his family and the slave community in the villain's power. A suppressed document transfers ownership of Terrebonne to M'Closky, absence of a signed document redefines Zoe as a slave, and a photograph confirms M'Closky to be a thief and murderer.

Another common melodramatic plot device is the villain's use of the circumstance of mortgage or rent payments in arrears as a pretext for displacing the hero and heroine both from place and from social status. Marjorie Howes notes that property "is not simply an important theme for Boucicault; it provides a principle of organization for plot twists and a descriptive vocabulary for the heightened states of emotion that mark melodrama." As Howes also points out, in Boucicault's use of the "mortgage melodrama," "a mortgage is not simply an economic arrangement, but rather denotes a state of affairs that is at once economic, sexual, and personal." In this, Boucicault is very much a writer of his time; property plays a central role in British melodramas spanning the century, such as Douglas Jerrold's *Black-Ey'd Susan* (1829), Tom Taylor's *The Ticket-of-Leave Man* (1863), Henry Arthur Jones's *The Silver King* (1882), and indeed, in many of Boucicault's own plays, such as *The Colleen Bawn*. John Walker's *The Factory Lad* (1832) is one of many British melodramas to suggest that factory workers are, in effect, treated as the property of the factory owner. It is only a short step from the metaphoric representation of the factory worker as a piece of property to the literal reality of the condition of the slave in America.

It is a feature of melodrama as a genre that injustice must be acknowledged and that "correct" identifications of moral position and social status be scrupulously made by the play's end. Frequently, melodramas feature some sort of trial, however *ad hoc*, during which the wrong person is initially accused. This accusation is then dramatically overturned by a last-minute discovery made by the Comic Man, and the real villain is unmasked, named, and punished. In earlier plays, the Comic Man himself was typically a key witness; he would identify the villain to the crowd. By 1859, Boucicault was able to take advantage of a new technological marvel, the photograph, to provide more objective proof of the villain's identity.

The original version of *The Octoroon* deviated from the typical melodrama in one very important respect: it had a tragic ending. As the reviews in the Appendix show, London reviewers forcefully criticized Boucicault's choice to violate British audiences' expectations of the melodramatic genre, which, along with the expulsion (by death, exile, or prison) of the villain and a recovery and recognition of the characters' correct places in the world, requires a happy reunion of lovers at the end.

Scott Boltwood points out that in illustrations representing the famous slave auction scene, Zoe is differentiated from the other slaves, who have dark skin and are in ragged clothes. In the illustration reproduced on the cover of this volume, for example, Zoe is pale, dressed in a fashionable hoop skirt, and otherwise neat in her appearance, while the other objects of the auction are shadowy, dejected figures melting into the background. Lighter cross-hatching in the drawing of her figure and of her light-colored dress emphasize her whiteness; she stands out even from the other Caucasian figures.

Such contemporaneous representations of Zoe as a comfortably familiar, visibly Caucasian and middle-class young woman may help to explain why audiences, especially in England, felt particularly sympathetic towards her. Boucicault's choice to avoid any outward appearance of difference from the audience may be interpreted in more than one way: while he may have deliberately emphasized her Caucasian appearance to underscore the injustice of her position, he is just as likely to have understood that his audiences, whether conservative or liberal, would find it more difficult to connect with the plight of a heroine who looked alien.

Even though she is physically indistinguishable from the other white characters, Zoe is treated as an in-between figure in the racial divisions in plantation society; though she is not abused, she is treated as a poor relation rather than an equal. Zoe is doubly an outsider in this society, due to her illegitimate birth as well as her racial origins. She has also been educated "beyond her station" (a situation very familiar to Victorian playgoers and readers). She is clearly more refined in her manners and her language than the slaves—and more refined as well than white characters such as the two overseers, Scudder and M'Closky. She is scrupulously honest in insisting on revealing her racial origins to George, even though she is convinced that by doing so she will end all possibility of his marrying her. Miscegenation laws made marriage between races illegal in Louisiana and several other states in the South,[1] but Zoe's expectation that George will reject her

---

1   The prohibition of interracial marriage remained in place in several Southern states well into the twentieth century. Louisiana overturned this law in response to a Supreme Court decision in 1967; Alabama's miscegenation law remained valid until 2000.

is not only a matter of Louisiana's laws. A sense of the inferiority of her racial makeup is deeply ingrained in her, as it is in the other slaves, such as Pete and Paul.

Native Americans in *The Octoroon*

Although Zoe is the central figure in this play, other characters also represent positions of racial otherness. Perhaps the most unexpected character in this play is Wahnotee, the "Lepan" chief. The Lepans, commonly known as the Lipan Apache people, had a long history of displacement caused by hostile action both by white Americans and by other Native American groups. By the end of the eighteenth century, most Texas Lipans had been forced to join other Apache groups in Mexico. Those who were still in Texas worked with the white settlers as scouts and trading partners, often protecting those settlers from hostile Native American groups. But despite their part in supporting the Americans in the Mexican-American war, they were not regarded as allies. The Texans established a campaign of extermination; those who survived were exiled to Mexico. Though Wahnotee is a "chief," he appears to be an isolated exile in Louisiana.

As the character who avenges the innocent boy and saves society from the villain's machinations, Wahnotee is given a heroic role. Boucicault's initial choice to play him, rather than the secondary hero, Scudder, or even the villain, M'Closky, suggests that Wahnotee was a particularly significant character for the playwright, and that he was performed sympathetically. Perhaps, however, Wahnotee is merely another version of the "noble savage" who populated the adventure tales of the Old West and other colonialist narratives in popular literature. Wahnotee does possess many stereotypical qualities: though he is given some heroic status, he also carries a tomahawk, is a drunkard, and can usually manage only an "Ugh" in response to complicated questions. Even the slave child is more articulate; he serves as an interpreter between Wahnotee and the plantation society.

While castigating him for his drunkenness, and using the same type of insulting language used by Pete, Paul nevertheless shows Wahnotee a tenderness and protectiveness that is reciprocated. This is an unusual relationship for a variety of reasons. There were very few popular American melodramas that described friendships between

Native American characters and white Americans;[1] friendship between slaves and Native American peoples was an even rarer topic in melodrama. There were certainly accounts of friendly and honorable Native American characters in memoirs and in literary works, such as Henry Wadsworth Longfellow's *Song of Hiawatha* or James Fenimore Cooper's *The Last of the Mohicans*. However, the more common perception of most Native peoples was that they were savages who would kill any stranger. (It is important to remember that the above-mentioned works of fiction or non-fiction prose were all written by non-Native authors, and that even the most positive portrayals often drew on the "noble savage" stereotype.)

The terms of friendship between Paul and Wahnotee are also unusual. Friendship between a child and an unrelated adult is often formulated as a relationship between an adult mentor and a child who may be coming of age, but here, the friendship appears to be on more even terms. The Native American character is portrayed as childlike himself in his enjoyment of the simple pleasures he shares with Paul, while Paul takes on a more adult role as he instructs Wahnotee both in "civilized" behavior and in modern technology. However, after Paul's death, Wahnotee becomes progressively more "adult" as he is able to communicate with the plantation community, demonstrating some ability with the "mash-up" or mixture of languages spoken in Louisiana. He also exhibits the bloodthirstiness and warrior-like qualities expected of the "Indian chief" (to different degrees, according to the variations in the play's endings) in the climactic attack on M'Closky.

The Octoroon's Influences on Later Work

The Octoroon has been seen as the direct precursor of the Irish plays for which Boucicault was best known in England and Ireland. *The Colleen Bawn*, which was written almost directly after *The Octoroon*, also featured a helpless heroine oppressed by an evil member of the ruling class—this time, the English—and loved by another member

---

1   Two well-known examples are James Nelson Barker's romantic play *The Indian Princess* (1808), about Pocahontas and Captain John Smith, and John Augustus Stone's *Metamora, Or the Last of the Wampanoags* (1824), a tragic tale about the "noble savage" or "natural gentleman," Metamora.

of the ruling class. The two plays were performed concurrently at New York's Laura Keene Theatre and later in a double bill in London.

The Octoroon was revived at the Royal Theatre Stratford East in 1885, a theater with a continuing tradition of producing plays that engage with issues of race and oppression. A film of *The Octoroon* made in 1912 in Sydney, Australia,[1] reflected the interest of many Australians in challenging the racial divisions in their own country. In 1913, the Kalem Company in America also made a film of the play; when the film magazine *Moving Picture World* enthusiastically reviewed the most sensational scenes, the off-stage death of M'Closky was particularly appreciated:

> Exciting indeed is the chase of the overseer by the Indian. It is with considerable suspense that we watched the frantic flight of the overseer and the stealthy trailing of his victim by the avenger. We were not permitted to witness the final struggle in its entirety, but a white clutching hand, trembling for a moment above the reeds of a swamp, and presently the appearance of the Indian wiping his knife tells the story of vengeance accomplished.[2]

Twenty-first-century productions of the play—such as American playwright Branden Jacobs-Jenkins's off-Broadway adaptation in 2010 (revived in 2014), and British playwright Mark Ravenhill's 2013 BBC radio adaptation, taped in front of a live audience at the same theater where it had been revived in 1885—continue to demonstrate the power of this melodrama to arouse fundamental emotions and prompt a deep engagement with issues of oppression and injustice.

Note on the Spelling of the Author's Name

All references to Boucicault's name in the US use the alternative spelling of "Bourcicault," a spelling sometimes used by the author himself, if we may take letters to newspaper editors as evidence.

---

1   *The Octoroon*. Directed by George Young. Sydney: Australian Film Syndicate, 1912.
2   "The Octoroon." Review. *Moving Picture World*, 15 November 1913, 716.

A Note on the Text

The Octoroon evolved in several stages, as a result of which there are several different versions of the play. In the original American version, reproduced here, the play has five acts and ends with Zoe's suicide.[1] Other versions provide a more melodramatic, spectacular ending, including M'Closky's kidnapping of Zoe, a frantic chase led by Scudder to rescue Zoe, a boat explosion, M'Closky's death at the hands of Wahnotee—either described clearly or enacted onstage—and a brief account (often in stage directions) either of Zoe's suicide or of the averting of that suicide. In the versions that focus on the spectacular chase and explosion, Zoe's suicide scene is moved to the penultimate scene instead of the final one. In some versions of the play, various scenes of confrontation between M'Closky and Zoe, Wahnotee, or Scudder are expanded. Some versions are in three acts, some in four, and others in five. The change that appeared the most significant to audiences and reviewers in Britain was the reprieve of Zoe, who in some versions does not commit suicide after all. In a novella adaptation of the play, the happy ending is expanded upon to tidy up all loose ends: not only does Zoe live, but she also marries and has children with George Peyton. Mrs. Peyton overcomes her prejudice and even Dora and Salem are paired off.

The text of this edition is based on that of the original five-act American edition. The earliest printed version appears to be a privately printed edition (the Fisk University copy of which is available online). That edition does not list either a place or a date of publication. Some have assigned a tentative date of 1861; John A. Degen in a 1975 article in *The Educational Theatre Journal* has argued plausibly for a date of 1859.

A frequently referenced text of the play is that published in *Representative American Plays*, a large anthology edited by Arthur Hobson Quinn, first published in 1917. Quinn states that the text used for his anthology is "a reprint of the privately printed edition," but (as Degen has pointed out) Quinn altered the stage directions substantially. It is true that the stage directions in the first American printed edition

---

1   For selections from and descriptions of other versions, see the contextual materials included at the end of this volume.

are not as extensive as they might be; for that reason the present text follows the example of Peter Thomson's Cambridge University Press edition (1984) in drawing as well on the texts of early editions published in the UK—notably, the Dick's Standard Plays #391 edition (London, no date)—with their fuller stage directions.

Despite the changed ending (and the associated change from a five-act to a four-act structure), the dialogue as presented in early British editions—among them the Dick's, and also the Lacy's Acting Edition, #963, London, no date—is very much the same as in the first American one. Unlike Thomson in his Cambridge edition of five Boucicault plays, the present edition has maintained the spellings of the first American edition. These are the same as the American spellings of today in most respects—but not in all. The change that Noah Webster had inspired was not yet complete in the late 1850s; the first American text has *color*, *favorite*, and *neighbors*—but also *fibre* and *programme*.

The Octoroon;[1] or, Life in Louisiana

Characters in the Play:

GEORGE PEYTON, *Mrs. Peyton's nephew, educated in Europe, and just returned home*

JACOB M'CLOSKY, *formerly overseer of Terrebonne, but now owner of one half of the estate*

SALEM SCUDDER, *a Yankee from Massachusetts, now overseer of Terrebonne, great on improvements and inventions, once a photographic operator, and been a little of everything generally*

PETE, *an "Ole Uncle," once the late judge's body servant, but now "too ole to work, sa."*

SUNNYSIDE, *a planter[2]*

LAFOUCHE, *a rich planter*

PAUL, *a yellow boy,[3] a favorite of the late judge's, and so allowed to do much as he likes*

RATTS, *captain of the Magnolia Steamer*

COLONEL POINTDEXTER, *an auctioneer*

JULES THIBODEAUX, *a young Creole[4] planter*

CAILLOU, *an overseer*

JUDGE JACKSON, *a planter*

CLAIBORNE, *the auctioneer's clerk*

SOLON, *a slave*

WAHNOTEE, *an Indian chief of the Lepan tribe[5]*

MRS. PEYTON, *widow of the late judge*

ZOE, *an Octoroon girl, free*

DORA SUNNYSIDE, *a southern belle*

GRACE, *a yellow girl, a slave*

---

1   *Octoroon*   Person who is one-eighth black and seven-eighths white. Boucicault is generally credited with having invented this term. The term used for one who was one-quarter black was quadroon; the term for one who was half black, mulatto. (All three terms are now considered offensive.)

2   *planter*   Plantation owner.

3   *a yellow boy*   The term "yellow" refers to the light or golden skin tone of mixed-race slaves. The original English and American productions, and many nineteenth-century productions of the play, followed the tradition of casting a girl to play a young boy.

4   *Creole*   Native of Louisiana, of French, Spanish, or mixed ancestry.

5   *Lepan tribe*   The Lepan people were located in Texas.

DIDO, *the cook, a slave*
MRS. CLAIBORNE
MINNIE, *a quadroon slave*
CHILDREN

Act i

(*A view of the plantation Terrebonne, in Louisiana. A branch of the Mississippi is seen winding through the Estate. A low-built but extensive planter's dwelling, surrounded with a verandah and raised a few feet from the ground, occupies the left side—a table and chairs, right centre.* GRACE *discovered sitting at breakfast table with* CHILDREN. *Enter* SOLON *from house.*)

SOLON. Yah! you bomn'ble fry[1]—git out—a gen'lman can't pass for you.

GRACE. (*Seizing a fly whisk.*) Hee! ha—git out! (*Drives* CHILDREN *away—in escaping they tumble against and trip up* SOLON, *who falls with a tray—the* CHILDREN *steal the bananas and rolls that fall about. Enter* PETE *(he is lame)—he carries a mop and pail.*)

PETE. Hey! laws a massey![2] why, clar[3] out! drop dat banana! I'll murder dis yer[4] crowd. (*He chases* CHILDREN *about—they leap over railing at back. Exit* SOLON.) Dem little niggers[5] is a judgment upon dis generation.

(*Enter* GEORGE *from house.*)

GEORGE. What's the matter, Pete?
PETE. It's dem black trash, Mas'r[6] George; dis 'ere property wants claring—dem's too numerous round; when I gets time, I'll kill some on[7] 'em, sure!
GEORGE. They don't seem to be scared by the threat.

---

1 *bomn'ble fry* Abominable children (small fry). Insulting language appears to function as an indication of affection and intimacy within the slave community.
2 *laws a massey* Colloquialism, from "Lord's a mercy."
3 *clar* Clear.
4 *yer* Here.
5 *niggers* This derogatory term (a corruption of "negroes") remained in frequent use by many white Americans in the South until well into the 1960s.
6 *Mas'r* Master.
7 *on* Of.

PETE. 'Top, you varmin![1] 'top till I get enough of you in one place!

GEORGE. Were they all born on this estate?

PETE. Guess they nebber[2] was born—dem tings! what dem?—get away! Born here—dem darkies? What, on Terrebonne! Don't believe it, Mas'r George—dem black tings never was born at all; dey swarmed one mornin' on a sassafras tree in the swamp—I cotched 'em, day ain't no count.[3] Don't b'lieve dey'll turn out niggers when dere growed—dey'll come out sunthin else.

GRACE. Yes, Mas'r George, dey was born here; and old Pete is fonder on 'em dan he is of his fiddle on a Sunday.

PETE. What? dem tings—dem?—get away. (*Makes blow at the* CHILDREN.) Born here! dem darkies! What on Terrebonne? Don't b'lieve it, Mas'r George—no. One mornin' they swarmed on a sassafras tree in de swamp, and I cotched 'em all in a sieve—dat's how dey come on top of dis yearth—git out, you—ya, ya! (*Laughs.*)

(*Exit* GRACE. *Enter* MRS. PEYTON, *from house.*)

MRS. P. So, Pete, you are spoiling those children as usual?

PETE. Dat's right, missus! gib[4] it to ole Pete! he's allers[5] in for it. Git away dere! Ya! if dey ain't all lighted[6] like coons[7] on dat snake fence,[8] just out of shot. Look dar! Dem debils.[9] Ya!

MRS. P. Pete! do you hear?

PETE. Git down dar! I'm arter[10] you! (*Hobbles off.*)

MRS. P. You are out early this morning, George.

GEORGE. I was up before daylight. We got the horses saddled, and galloped down the shell road over the Piney Patch then,

---

1 '*Top, you varmin!*   Stop, you vermin!
2 *nebber*   Never.
3 *I cotched … no count*   I caught them; they're of no account.
4 *gib*   Give.
5 *allers*   Always.
6 *lighted*   Alighted, sat on.
7 *coons*   Raccoons; also, nineteenth-century slang for African-Americans.
8 *snake fence*   Fence made of crossed rails laid out in a zigzag pattern; also called a "worm" or "Virginia fence."
9 *debils*   Devils.
10 *arter*   After.

coasting the Bayou Lake, we crossed the long swamps by Paul's Path, and so came home again.

MRS. P. (*Laughing.*) You seem already familiar with the name of every spot on the estate.

(*Enter* PETE—*arranges breakfast etc.*)

GEORGE. Just one month ago I quitted Paris. I left that siren city as I would have left a beloved woman.

MRS. P. No wonder! I dare say you left at least a dozen beloved women there, at the same time.

GEORGE. I feel that I departed amid universal and sincere regret. I left my loves and my creditors equally inconsolable.

MRS. P. George, you are incorrigible. Ah! you remind me so much of your uncle, the judge.

GEORGE. Bless his dear old handwriting, it's all I ever saw of him. For ten years his letters came every quarter day with a remittance, and a word of advice in his formal cavalier style; and then a joke in the postscript that upset the dignity of the foregoing. Aunt, when he died, two years ago, I read over those letters of his, and if I didn't cry like a baby—

MRS. P. No, George; say you wept like a man. And so you really kept those foolish letters?

GEORGE. Yes; I kept the letters, and squandered the money.

MRS. P. (*Embracing him.*) Ah! why were you not my son—you are so like my dear husband.

(*Enter* SALEM SCUDDER.)

SCUDDER. Ain't he! Yes—when I saw him and Miss Zoe galloping through the green sugar crop, and doing ten dollars' worth of damage at every stride, says I, how like his old uncle he do make the dirt fly.

GEORGE. Oh, aunt! what a bright, gay creature she is.

SCUDDER. What, Zoe! Guess that you didn't leave anything female in Europe that can lift an eyelash beside that gal. When she goes along, she just leaves a streak of love behind her. It's a good drink to see her come into the cottonfields—the niggers get fresh on the sight of her. If she ain't worth her weight in sunshine, you may take one of my fingers off, and choose which you like.

MRS. P. She need not keep us waiting breakfast, though. Pete, tell Miss Zoe that we are waiting.

PETE. Yes, missus. Why, Minnie, why don't you run when you hear, you lazy crittur?[1] (MINNIE *runs off.*) Dat's de laziest nigger on dis yere property. (*Sits down.*) Don't do nuffin.[2]

MRS. P. My dear George, you are left in your uncle's will heir to this estate.

GEORGE. Subject to your life-interest and an annuity to Zoe, is it not so?

MRS. P. I fear that the property is so involved that the strictest economy will scarcely recover it. My dear husband never kept any accounts, and we scarcely know in what condition the estate really is.

SCUDDER. Yes we do, ma'am; it's in a darned bad condition. Ten years ago the judge took as overseer a bit of Connecticut hardware called M'Closky. The judge didn't understand accounts—the overseer did. For a year or two all went fine. The judge drew money like bourbon whisky from a barrel, and never turned off the tap. But out it flew, free for everybody or anybody, to beg, borrow, or steal. So it went, till one day the judge found the tap wouldn't run. He looked in to see what stopped it, and pulled out a big mortgage. "Sign that," says the overseer, "it's only a formality." "All right," says the judge, and away went a thousand acres; so at the end of eight years, Jacob M'Closky, Esquire, finds himself proprietor of the richest half of Terrebonne

GEORGE. But the other half is free.

SCUDDER. No, it ain't, because, just then, what does the judge do but hire another overseer—a Yankee—a Yankee named Salem Scudder.

MRS.P. Oh, no, it was—

SCUDDER. Hold on now! I'm going to straighten this account clear out. What was this here Scudder? Well, he lived in New York by sittin' with his heels up in front of French's Hotel, and inventin'—

GEORGE. Inventing what?

---

1 *crittur* Creature.
2 *nuffin* Nothing.

SCUDDER. Improvements—anything from a staylace[1] to a fire engine. Well, he cut that for the photographing line. He and his apparatus arrived here, took the judge's likeness and his fancy, who made him overseer right off. Well, sir, what does this Scudder do but introduces his inventions and improvements on this estate. His new cotton gins[2] broke down, the steam sugar-mills burst up, until he finished off with folly what Mr. M'Closky with his knavery began.

MRS. P. Oh, Salem! how can you say so? Haven't you worked like a horse?

SCUDDER. No, ma'am, I worked like an ass—an honest one, and that's all. Now, Mr. George, between the two overseers, you and that good old lady have come to the ground; that is the state of things, just as near as I can fix it.

(ZOE *sings without.*)

GEORGE. 'Tis Zoe.

SCUDDER. Oh! I have not spoiled that anyhow. I can't introduce any darned improvement there. Ain't that a cure for old age; it kinder lifts the heart up, don't it?

MRS. P. Poor child! what will become of her when I am gone? If you haven't spoiled her, I fear I have. She has had the education of a lady.[3]

GEORGE. I have remarked that she is treated by the neighbors with a kind of familiar condescension that annoyed me.

SCUDDER. Do you know that she is the natural daughter[4] of the judge, your uncle, and that old lady thar[5] just adored anything he cared for; and this girl, that another woman would a hated, she loves as if she'd been her own child.

---

1   *staylace*   Lace used to bind a woman's corset.
2   *cotton gins*   Machines for cleaning seeds from raw cotton fiber.
3   *education of a lady*   The education of slaves was strongly discouraged, much as the education of the working classes had been discouraged in England; literacy was feared by American slave owners and English ruling classes as a path to advancement. Boucicault is entering a popular debate about the wisdom of educating people out of their "station in life"; the argument was that education created unhappiness when there were no opportunities for people to exercise their skills, and it could lead to dangerous ideas about upward mobility.
4   *natural daughter*   Illegitimate daughter.
5   *thar*   There.

GEORGE. Aunt, I am prouder and happier to be your nephew and heir to the ruins of Terrebonne than I would have been to have had half Louisiana without you.

(*Enter* ZOE, *from house.*)

ZOE. Am I late? Ah! Mr. Scudder, good morning.

SCUDDER. Thank'ye. I'm from fair to middlin', like a bamboo cane, much the same all the year round.

ZOE. No: like a sugar cane—so dry outside, one would never think there was so much sweetness within.

SCUDDER. Look here; I can't stand that gal! if I stop here, I shall hug her right off. (*Sees* PETE *who has set his pail down upstage, and goes to sleep on it.*) If that old nigger ain't asleep, I'm blamed. Hillo! (*Kicks pail from under* PETE, *and exit.*)

PETE. Hi! Debbel's in de pail! Whar's breakfass?[1]

(*Enter* SOLON *and* DIDO *with coffee pot, dishes, etc.*)

DIDO. Bless'ee, Missey Zoe, here it be. Dere's a dish of penpans— jess taste, Mas'r George—and here's fried bananas; smell 'em, do, sa glosh.

PETE. Hole yer tongue, Dido. Whar's de coffee? (*Pours out.*) If it don't stain de cup, your wicked ole life's in danger sure! dat right! black as nigger; clar as ice. You may drink dat, Mas'r George. (*Looks off.*) Ya! here's Mas'r Sunnyside, and Missey Dora, jist drov up. Some of you niggers, run and hole de hosses; and take dis, Dido. (*Gives her coffee pot to hold, and hobbles off, followed by* SOLON *and* DIDO.)

(*Enter* SUNNYSIDE *and* DORA.)

SUNNYSIDE. Good day, ma'am. (*Shakes hands with* GEORGE.) I see we are just in time for breakfast. (*Sits.*)

DORA. Oh, none for me; I never eat. (*Sits.*)

GEORGE. (*Aside.*) They do not notice Zoe. (*Aloud.*) You don't see Zoe, Mr. Sunnyside.

SUNNYSIDE. Ah! Zoe, girl; are you there!

DORA. Take my shawl, Zoe. (ZOE *helps her.*) What a good creature she is.

---

1 *Whar's breakfass?* Where's breakfast?

SUNNYSIDE. I dare say, now, that in Europe you have never met any lady more beautiful in person, or more polished in manners, than that girl.

GEORGE. You are right, sir; though I shrank from expressing that opinion in her presence, so bluntly.

SUNNYSIDE. Why so?

GEORGE. It may be considered offensive.

SUNNYSIDE. (*Astonished.*) What? I say, Zoe, do you hear that?

DORA. Mr. Peyton is joking.

MRS. P. My nephew is not yet acquainted with our customs in Louisiana, but he will soon understand.

GEORGE. Never, aunt! I shall never understand how to wound the feelings of any lady; and, if that is the custom here, I shall never acquire it.

DORA. Zoe, my dear, what does he mean?

ZOE. I don't know.

GEORGE. Excuse me, I'll light a cigar. (*Goes upstage.*)

DORA. (*Aside to* ZOE.) Isn't he sweet? Oh, dear Zoe, is he in love with anybody?

ZOE. How can I tell?

DORA. Ask him, I want to know; don't say I told you to enquire, but find out—Minnie, fan me, it is so nice—and his clothes are French, ain't they?

ZOE. I think so; shall I ask him that too?

DORA. No, dear. I wish he would make love[1] to me. When he speaks to one he does it so easy, so gentle, it isn't bar-room style—love lined with drinks, sighs tinged with tobacco—and they say all the women in Paris were in love with him, which I feel *I* shall be—stop fanning me—what nice boots he wears.

SUNNYSIDE. (*To* MRS. PEYTON.) Yes, ma'am, I hold a mortgage over Terrebonne, mine's a ninth, and pretty near covers all the property, except the slaves. I believe Mr. M'Closky has a bill of sale on them. Oh, here he is.

(*Enter* M'CLOSKY.)

---

1   *make love* Act in a romantic way. (Use of the term "make love" to mean "have sexual intercourse" dates from the mid-twentieth century.)

SUNNYSIDE. Good morning, Mr. M'Closky.

M'CLOSKY. Good morning, Mr. Sunnyside, Miss Dora, your servant.

DORA. (*Seated.*) Fan me, Minnie. (*Aside.*) I don't like that man.

M'CLOSKY. (*Aside.*) Insolent as usual. (*Aloud.*) You begged me to call this morning. I hope I'm not intruding.

MRS. P. My nephew, Mr. Peyton.

M'CLOSKY. Oh, how d'ye do, sir? (*Offers hand.* GEORGE *bows coldly. Aside.*) A puppy;[1] if he brings any of his European airs here we'll fix him. (*Aloud.*) Zoe, tell Pete to give my mare a feed, will ye?

GEORGE. (*Angrily.*) Sir!

M'CLOSKY. Hillo, did I tread on ye?

MRS. P. What is the matter with George?

ZOE. (*Taking fan from* MINNIE.) Go, Minnie, tell Pete, run!

(*Exit* MINNIE.)

MRS. P. Grace, attend to Mr. M'Closky.

M'CLOSKY. A julep,[2] gal, that's my breakfast, and a bit of cheese.

GEORGE. (*Aside to* MRS. PEYTON.) How can you ask that vulgar ruffian to your table?

MRS. P. Hospitality in Europe is a courtesy; here, it is an obligation. We tender food to a stranger, not because he is a gentleman, but because he is hungry.

GEORGE. Aunt, I will take my rifle down to the Atchafalaya.[3] Paul has promised me a bear and a deer or two. I see my little Nimrod[4] yonder, with his Indian companion. Excuse me, ladies. Ho! Paul! (*Enters house.*)

PAUL. (*Outside.*) I'ss,[5] Mas'r George. (*Enters with* WAHNOTEE.)

SUNNYSIDE. It's a shame to allow that young cub to run over the swamps and woods, hunting and fishing his life away instead of hoeing cane.

---

1 *puppy* Arrogant young man.
2 *julep* Sugary drink made from mint and bourbon or other liquor.
3 *Atchafalaya* River in Louisiana.
4 *Nimrod* Hunter. Cf. Genesis 10.8-12.
5 *I'ss* Yes.

Mrs. P. The child was a favorite of the judge, who encouraged his gambols. I couldn't bear to see him put to work.

George. (*Returning with rifle.*) Come, Paul, are you ready?

Paul. I'ss Mas'r George. Oh, golly! ain't that a pooty[1] gun.

M'Closky. See here, you imps; if I catch you and your redskin yonder gunning in my swamps, I'll give you rats, mind— them vagabonds, when the game's about, shoot my pigs.

(*Exit* George *into house.*)

Paul. You gib me ratten, Mas'r Clostry, but I guess you take a berry long stick to Wahnotee; ugh, he make bacon of you.

M'Closky. Make bacon of me, you young whelp. Do you mean that I'm a pig? Hold on a bit. (*Seizes whip and holds* Paul.)

Zoe. Oh, sir! don't, pray don't.

M'Closky. (*Slowly lowering his whip.*) Darn you, redskin,[2] I'll pay you off some day, both of ye. (*Returns to table and drinks.*)

Sunnyside. That Indian is a nuisance. Why don't he return to his nation out west?

M'Closky. He's too fond of thieving and whisky.

Zoe. No; Wahnotee is a gentle, honest creature, and remains here because he loves that boy with the tenderness of a woman. When Paul was taken down with the swamp fever the Indian sat outside the hut, and neither ate, slept, or spoke for five days, till the child could recognize and call him to his bedside. He who can love so well is honest—don't speak ill of poor Wahnotee.

Mrs. P. Wahnotee, will you go back to your people?

Wahnotee. Sleugh.

Paul. He don't understand; he speaks a mash up[3] of Indian, French and Mexican. Wahnotee Patira na sepau assa wigiran.

Wahnotee. Weal Omenee.

---

1 *pooty* Pretty.
2 *redskin* Native American person. This term is now considered racist and offensive.
3 *mash up* Combination. This is apparently the first recorded use of the term.

PAUL. Says he'll go if I'll go with him. He calls me Omenee,[1] the pigeon, and Miss Zoe is Ninemoosha,[2] the sweetheart.

WAHNOTEE. (*Pointing to* ZOE.) Ninemoosha.

ZOE. No, Wahnotee, we can't spare Paul.

PAUL. If Omenee remain, Wahnotee will die in Terrebonne.

(*During the dialogue* WAHNOTEE *has taken George's gun; enter* GEORGE.)

GEORGE. Now I'm ready. (*Tries to regain his gun;* WAHNOTEE *refuses to give it up;* PAUL *quietly takes it from him, and remonstrates with him.*)

DORA. Zoe, he's going; I want him to stay and make love to me— that's what I came for today.

MRS. P. George, I can't spare Paul for an hour or two; he must run over to the landing; the steamer from New Orleans passed up the river last night, and if there's a mail they have thrown it ashore.

SUNNYSIDE. I saw the mailbags lying in the shed this morning.

MRS. P. I expect an important letter from Liverpool; away with you, Paul, bring the mailbags here.

PAUL. I'm 'most[3] afraid to take Wahnotee to the shed, there's rum there.

WAHNOTEE. Rum!

PAUL. Come, then, but if I catch you drinkin', oh, laws a mussey,[4] you'll get snakes! I'll gib it you! now mind. (*Exit with* WAHNOTEE.)

GEORGE. Come, Miss Dora, let me offer you my arm.

DORA. Mr. George, I am afraid, if all we hear is true, you have led a dreadful life in Europe.

GEORGE. That's a challenge to begin a description of my feminine adventures.

---

1 *Omenee* Alternative spelling of Omemee, a word used by various Native American groups (including the Ojibwe and Massassagas) for pigeon.

2 *Ninemoosha* Alternative spelling of Nenemoosha, a name and meaning ("my sweetheart") used by Henry Wadsworth Longfellow in "The Son of the Evening Star," from *The Song of Hiawatha* (1855).

3 *'most* Almost.

4 *laws a mussey* Lord have mercy.

DORA. You have been in love, then?

GEORGE. Two hundred and forty-nine times! let me relate you the worst cases.

DORA. No! no!

GEORGE. I'll put the naughty parts in French.

DORA. I won't hear a word! Oh, you horrible man! go on.

(*Exit* GEORGE *and* DORA *to house.*)

M'CLOSKY. Now, ma'am I'd like a little business if agreeable. I bring you news: your banker, old La Fouche, of New Orleans, is dead; the executors are winding up his affairs, and have foreclosed on all overdue mortgages, so Terrebonne is for sale. Here's the *Picayune*[1] (*Producing paper.*) with the advertisement.

ZOE. Terrebonne for sale!

MRS. P. Terrebonne for sale, and you, sir, will doubtless become its purchaser.

M'CLOSKY. Well, ma'am I spose there's no law agin[2] my bidding for it. The more bidders, the better for you. You'll take care, I guess, it don't go too cheap.

MRS. P. Oh, sir, I don't value the place for its price, but for the many happy days I've spent here; that landscape, flat and uninteresting though it may be, is full of charm for me; those poor people, born around me, growing up about my heart, have bounded my view of life; and now to lose that homely[3] scene, lose their black ungainly faces,—oh, sir, perhaps you should be as old as I am to feel as I do when my past life is torn away from me.

M'CLOSKY. I'd be darned glad if somebody would tear my past life away from *me.* Sorry I can't help you, but the fact is you're in such an all-fired mess that you couldn't be pulled out without a derrick.[4]

---

1 *Picayune* Louisiana newspaper; also the name of a five cent coin. Some of Boucicault's letters concerning *The Octoroon* and published in the *Picayune* can be found in this edition's appendix.
2 *agin* Against.
3 *homely* Homey; cozy.
4 *derrick* Crane for moving or lifting heavy weights.

Mrs. P. Yes, there is a hope left yet, and I cling to it. The house of Mason Brothers, of Liverpool, failed some twenty years ago in my husband's debt.

M'Closky. They owed him over 50,000 dollars.

Mrs. P. I cannot find the entry in my husband's accounts, but you, Mr. M'Closky, can doubtless detect it. Zoe, bring here the judge's old desk; it is in the library.

(*Exit* Zoe *to house.*)

M'Closky. You don't expect to recover any of this old debt, do you?

Mrs. P. Yes, the firm has recovered itself, and I received a notice two months ago that some settlement might be anticipated.

Sunnyside. Why, with principal and interest this debt has been more than doubled in twenty years.

Mrs. P. But it may be years yet before it will be paid off, if ever.

Sunnyside. If there's a chance of it, there's not a planter round here who wouldn't lend you the whole cash, to keep your name and blood amongst us. Come, cheer up, old friend.

Mrs. P. Ah! Sunnyside, how good you are—so like my poor Peyton.

(*Exit* Mrs. Peyton *and* Sunnyside *to house.*)

M'Closky. Curse their old families—they cut me—a bilious, conceited, thin lot of dried up aristocracy. I hate 'em. Just because my grandfather wasn't some broken-down Virginia transplant, or a stingy old Creole, I ain't fit to sit down to the same meat with them—it makes my blood so hot I feel my heart hiss. I'll sweep these Peytons from this section of the country. Their presence keeps alive the reproach against me, that I ruined them; yet, if this money should come. Bah! There's no chance of it. Then, if they go they'll take Zoe— she'll follow them. Darn that girl, she makes me quiver when I think of her; she's took me for all I'm worth.

(*Enter* Zoe *from house, with the desk.*)

Oh, here! do you know what the annuity the old judge left you is worth today? not a picayune.

ZOE. It's surely worth the love that dictated it; here are the papers and accounts. (*Putting it on the table.*)

M'CLOSKY. Stop, Zoe; come here! How would you like to rule the house of the richest planter on Atchapalaga[1]—eh? or say the word, and I'll buy this old barrack, and you shall be mistress of Terrebonne.

ZOE. Oh, sir, do not speak so to me!

M'CLOSKY. Why not? Look here, these Peytons are bust, cut 'em; I am rich, jine[2] me; I'll set you up grand, and we'll give these first families here our dust, until you'll see their white skins shrivel up with hate and rage; what d'ye say?

ZOE. Let me pass! Oh, pray, let me go!

M'CLOSKY. What, you won't, won't ye? If young George Peyton was to make you the same offer, you'd jump at it pretty darned quick, I guess. Come, Zoe, don't be a fool, I'd marry you if I could, but you know I can't,[3] so just say what you want. Here, then, I'll put back these Peytons in Terrebonne, and they shall know you done it; yes, they'll have you to thank for saving them from ruin.

ZOE. Do you think they would live here on such terms?

M'CLOSKY. Why not? We'll hire out our slaves, and live on their wages.

ZOE. But I'm not a slave.

M'CLOSKY. No, if you were I'd buy you, if you cost all I'm worth.

ZOE. Let me pass!

M'CLOSKY. Stop!

(*Enter* SCUDDER.)

SCUDDER. Let her pass!

M'CLOSKY. Eh?

SCUDDER. Let her pass! (*Takes out his knife. Exit* ZOE *to house.*)

M'CLOSKY. Is that you, Mr. Overseer? (*Examines paper.*)

SCUDDER. Yes, I'm here somewhere, interferin'.

---

1 *Atchapalaga* Alternative spelling of Atchafalaya, a river and river basin located in Louisiana.
2 *jine* Join.
3 *I'd marry you … I can't* Miscegenation laws in Louisiana made interracial marriage illegal.

M'CLOSKY. (*Sitting.*) A pretty mess you've got this estate in—

SCUDDER. Yes—me and Co.—we done it; but, as you were senior partner in the concern, I reckon you got the big lick.

M'CLOSKY. What d'ye mean?

SCUDDER. Let me proceed by illustration. (*Sits.*) Look thar! (*Points with his knife off.*) D'ye see that tree? It's called a live oak, and is a native here; beside it grows a creeper; year after year that creeper twines its long arms round and round the tree— sucking the earth dry all about its roots—living on its life— over-running its branches, until at last the live oak withers and dies out.[1] Do you know what the niggers round here call that sight? They call it the Yankee hugging the Creole. (*Sits.*)

M'CLOSKY. Mr. Scudder, I've listened to a great many of your insinuations, and now I'd like to come to an understanding what they mean. If you want a quarrel—

SCUDDER. No, I'm the skurriest crittur[2] at a fight you ever see; my legs have been too well brought up to stand and see my body abused; I take good care of myself, I can tell you.

M'CLOSKY. Because I heard that you had traduced[3] my character.

SCUDDER. Traduced! Whoever said so lied. I always said you were the darndest thief that ever escaped a white jail to misrepresent the North to the South.

M'CLOSKY. (*Raising hand to back of his neck.*) What!

SCUDDER. Take your hand down—take it down. (M'CLOSKY *lowers his hand.*) Whenever I gets into company like yours, I always start with the advantage on my side.

M'CLOSKY. What d'ye mean?

SCUDDER. I mean that before you could draw that bowie knife[4] you wear down your back, I'd cut you into shingles. Keep quiet, and let's talk sense. You wanted to come to an understanding, and I'm coming thar as quick as I can. Now,

---

1   *D'ye see that tree ... dies out*   The metaphor of the ivy and the oak was also commonly applied to the relationship between a man and a woman in nineteenth-century popular discourse, with the woman functioning as the parasitic ivy draining the energy and spirit of the strong oak.
2   *skurriest crittur*   Most frightened creature.
3   *traduced*   Disgraced.
4   *bowie knife*   Hunting knife.

Jacob M'Closky, you despise me because you think I'm a fool; I despise you because I know you to be a knave. Between us we've ruined these Peytons; you fired the judge, and I finished off the widow. Now, I feel bad about my share in the business. I'd give half the balance of my life to wipe out my part of the work. Many a night I've laid awake and thought how to pull them through, till I've cried like a child over the sum I couldn't do; and you know how darned hard 'tis to make a Yankee cry.

M'CLOSKY. Well, what's that to me?

SCUDDER. Hold on, Jacob, I'm coming to that; I tell ye, I'm such a fool—I can't bear the feeling, it keeps at me like a skin complaint, and if this family is sold up—

M'CLOSKY. What then?

SCUDDER. (*Rising.*) I'd cut my throat—or yours—yours I'd prefer.

M'CLOSKY. Would you now? Why don't you do it?

SCUDDER. 'Cos I's skeered[1] to try! I never killed a man in my life—and civilization is so strong in me I guess I couldn't do it—I'd like to, though!

M'CLOSKY. And all for the sake of that old woman and that young puppy, eh? No other cause to hate—to envy me—to be jealous of me—eh?

SCUDDER. Jealous! what for?

M'CLOSKY. Ask the color in your face; d'ye think I can't read you like a book? With your New England hypocrisy, you would persuade yourself it was this family alone you cared for: it ain't—you know it ain't—'tis the "Octoroon," and you love her as I do, and you hate me because I'm your rival. That's where the tears come from, Salem Scudder, if you ever shed any—that's where the shoe pinches.

SCUDDER. Wal, I do like the gal; she's a—

M'CLOSKY. She's in love with young Peyton; it made me curse—whar it made you cry, as it does now. I see the tears on your cheeks now.

SCUDDER. Look at 'em, Jacob, for they are honest water from the well of truth. I ain't ashamed of it—I do love the gal; but I

---

1 *skeered* Scared.

ain't jealous of you, because I believe the only sincere feeling about you is your love for Zoe, and it does your heart good to have her image thar; but I believe you put it thar to spile.[1] By fair means I don't think you can get her, and don't you try foul with her, 'cause if you do, Jacob, civilization be darned, I'm on you like a painter,[2] and when I'm drawed out I'm pizin.[3] (*Exit to house.*)

M'CLOSKY. Fair or foul, I'll have her—take that home with you! (*Opens desk.*) What's here? Judgments? Yes, plenty of 'em; bill of costs; account with Citizen's Bank. What's this? "Judgment 40,000, Thibodeaux against Peyton"; surely that is the judgment under which this estate is now advertised for sale. (*Takes up paper and examines it.*) Yes, "Thibodeaux against Peyton, 1838." Hold on! whew! this is worth taking to. In this desk the judge used to keep one paper I want—this should be it. (*Reads.*) "The free papers of my daughter, Zoe, registered February 4th, 1841." Why, Judge, wasn't you lawyer enough to know that while a judgment stood against you, it was a lien[4] on your slaves? Zoe is your child by a quadroon slave, and you didn't free her. Blood! if this is so, she's mine! This old Liverpool debt—that may cross me. If it only arrive too late—if it don't come by this mail. Hold on! this letter the old lady expects—that's it: let me only head off that letter, and Terrebonne will be sold before they can recover it. That boy and the Indian have gone down to the landing for the postbags; they'll idle on the way as usual; my mare will take me across the swamp, and before they can reach the shed, I'll have purified them bags. Ne'er a letter shall show this mail. Ha, ha! (*Calls.*) Pete, you old turkey buzzard, saddle my mare. Then, if I sink every dollar I'm worth in her purchase, I'll own that Octoroon. (*Stands with his hand extended toward the house, and tableau.*)

---

1 *spile*   Spoil.
2 *painter*   Panther.
3 *pizin*   Poison.
4 *lien*   Bond that gives the debtor rights to the property of the person who owes the debt.

Act 2

(*The Wharf—goods, boxes, and bales scattered about—a camera on stand.* SCUDDER, DORA, GEORGE, *and* PAUL *discovered;* DORA *being photographed by* SCUDDER, *who is arranging photographic apparatus;* GEORGE *and* PAUL *looking on at back.*)

SCUDDER. Just turn your face a leetle this way—fix your—let's see—look here.

DORA. So?

SCUDDER. That's right. (*Puts his head under the darkening apron.*) It's such a long time since I did this sort of thing, and this old machine has got so dirty and stiff, I'm afraid it won't operate. That's about right. Now don't stir.

PAUL. Ugh! she look as though she war gwine[1] to have a tooth drawed!

SCUDDER. I've got four plates ready, in case we miss the first shot. One of them is prepared with a self-developing liquid that I've invented. I hope it will turn out better than most of my notions. Now fix yourself. Are you ready?

DORA. Ready!

SCUDDER. Fire!—one, two, three. (*Takes out watch.*)

PAUL. Now it's cooking. Laws mussey, I feel it all inside, as if I was at a lottery.

SCUDDER. So! (*Throws down apron.*) That's enough. (*Withdraws slide, turns and sees* PAUL.) What! what are you doing there, you young varmint? Ain't you took them bags to the house yet?

PAUL. Now, it ain't no use trying to get mad, Mas'r Scudder. I'm gwine! I only come back to find Wahnotee; whar is dat ign'ant[2] Ingiun?

SCUDDER. You'll find him scenting round the rum store, hitched up by the nose. (*Exit into room.*)

PAUL. (*Calling at door.*) Say, Mas'r Scudder, take me in dat telescope?

---

1 *war gwine* Was going.
2 *ign'ant* Ignorant.

SCUDDER. (*Inside room.*) Get out, you cub! clar out!

PAUL. You got four ob[1] dem dishes ready. Gosh, wouldn't I like to hav myself took! What's de charge, Mas'r Scudder? (*Runs off.*)

SCUDDER. (*Entering from room.*) Job had none of them critters on his plantation, else he'd never ha' stood through so many chapters. Well, that has come out clear, ain't it? (*Shows plate.*)

DORA. Oh, beautiful! Look, Mr. Peyton.

GEORGE. (*Looking.*) Yes, very fine!

SCUDDER. The apparatus can't mistake. When I travelled round with this machine, the homely folks used to sing out, "Hillo, mister this ain't like me!" "Ma'am," says I, "the apparatus can't mistake." "But, mister, that ain't my nose." "Ma'am, your nose drawed it. The machine can't err—you may mistake your phiz,[2] but the apparatus don't." "But, sir, it ain't agreeable." "No, ma'am, the truth seldom is."

(*Enter* PETE, *puffing.*)

PETE. Mas'r Scudder! Mas'r Scudder!

SCUDDER. Hillo! what are you blowing about like a steamboat with one wheel for?

PETE. You blow, Massa Scudder, when I tole you; dere's a man from Noo Aleens[3] just arriv' at de house, and he's stuck up two papers on de gates; "For sale—dis yer property," and a heap of oder[4] tings—and he seen missus, and arter[5] he shown some papers she burst out crying—I yelled; den de corious[6] of little niggers dey set up, den de hull[7] plantation children—de live stock reared up and created a purpiration of lamentation[8] as did de ole heart good to har.[9]

---

1 *ob* Of.
2 *phiz* Face.
3 *Noo Aleens* New Orleans.
4 *oder* Other.
5 *arter* After.
6 *den de corious* Then the chorus.
7 *hull* Whole.
8 *purpiration of lamentation* Suspiration or sigh of lamentation. Malapropisms were common in the representation of working class (or here, slave) characters, to emphasize their lack of education and signal the difference from the intellectual capacities of ruling class characters.
9 *har* Hear.

DORA. What's the matter?

SCUDDER. He's come.

PETE. Dass[1] it—I saw'm!

SCUDDER. The sheriff from New Orleans has taken possession—
Terrebonne is in the hands of the law.

(*Enter* ZOE.)

ZOE. Oh, Mr. Scudder! Dora! Mr. Peyton! come home—there are
strangers in the house.

DORA. Stay, Mr. Peyton; Zoe, a word! (*Leads her forward—aside.*)
Zoe, the more I see of George Peyton the better I like him;
but he is too modest—that is a very impertinent virtue in a
man.

ZOE. I'm no judge, dear.

DORA. Of course not, you little fool; no one ever made love to
you, and you can't understand. I mean that George knows I
am an heiress; my fortune would release this estate from debt.

ZOE. Oh, I see!

DORA. If he would only propose to marry me I would accept him,
but he don't know that, and he will go on fooling in his slow
European way until it is too late.

ZOE. What's to be done?

DORA. You tell him.

ZOE. What? that he isn't to go on fooling in his slow—

DORA. No, you goose! twit[2] him on his silence and abstraction—
I'm sure it's plain enough, for he has not spoken two words to
me all the day; then joke round the subject, and at last speak
out.

SCUDDER. Pete, as you came here did you pass Paul and the Indian
with the letter bags?

PETE. No, sar;[3] but dem vagabonds neber take de 'specable[4]
straight road, dey goes by de swamp. (*Exit up path.*)

SCUDDER. Come, sir!

DORA. (*To* ZOE.) Now's your time. (*Aloud.*) Mr. Scudder, take us

---

1 *Dass* That's.
2 *twit* Tease.
3 *sar* Sir.
4 *'specable* Respectable.

with you—Mr. Peyton is so slow, there's no getting him on.

(*Exit* DORA *and* SCUDDER.)

ZOE. They are gone! (*Glancing at* GEORGE.) Poor fellow, he has lost all.

GEORGE. Poor child! how sad she looks now she has no resource.

ZOE. How shall I ask him to stay?

GEORGE. Zoe, will you remain here? I wish to speak to you.

ZOE. (*Aside.*) Well, that saves trouble.

GEORGE. By our ruin, you lose all.

ZOE. Oh, I'm nothing; think of yourself.

GEORGE. I can think of nothing but the image that remains face to face with me: so beautiful, so simple, so confiding—that I dare not express the feelings that have grown up so rapidly in my heart.

ZOE. (*Aside.*) He means Dora.

GEORGE. If I dared to speak!

ZOE. That's just what you must do, and do it at once, or it will be too late.

GEORGE. Has my love been divined?

ZOE. It has been more than suspected.

GEORGE. Zoe, listen to me then—I shall see this estate pass from me without a sigh, for it possesses no charm for me; the wealth I covet is the love of those around me—eyes that are rich in fond looks—lips that breathe endearing words; the only estate I value is the heart of one true woman, and the slaves I'd have are her thoughts.

ZOE. George, George, your words take away my breath!

GEORGE. The world, Zoe, the free struggle of minds and hands is before me; the education bestowed on me by my dear uncle is a noble heritage which no sheriff can seize; with that I can build up a fortune, spread a roof over the heads I love, and place before them the food I have earned; I will work—

ZOE. Work! I thought none but colored people worked.

GEORGE. Work, Zoe, is the salt that gives flavor to life.

ZOE. Dora said you were slow—if she could hear you now—

GEORGE. Zoe, you are young; your mirror must have told you that you are beautiful. Is your heart free?

ZOE. Free? Of course it is!

GEORGE. We have known each other but a few days, but to me those days have been worth all the rest of my life. Zoe, you have suspected the feeling that now commands an utterance— you have seen that I love you.

ZOE. Me! you love me?

GEORGE. As my wife—the sharer of my hopes, my ambitions, and my sorrows; under the shelter of your love I could watch the storms of fortune pass unheeded by.

ZOE. *My* love! *My* love? George, you know not what you say. *I* the sharer of your sorrows—your wife. Do you know what I am?

GEORGE. Your birth—I know it. Has not my dear aunt forgotten it—she who had the most right to remember it? You are illegitimate, but love knows no prejudice.

ZOE. (*Aside.*) Alas! he does not know, he does not know! and will despise me, spurn me, loathe me, when he learns who, what he has so loved. (*Aloud.*) George, oh! forgive me! Yes, I love you—I did not know it until your words showed me what has been in my heart; each of them awoke a new sense, and now I know how unhappy—how very unhappy I am.

GEORGE. Zoe, what have I said to wound you?

ZOE. Nothing; but you must learn what I thought you already knew. George, you cannot marry me, the laws forbid it!

GEORGE. Forbid it?

ZOE. There is a gulf between us, as wide as your love—as deep as my despair; but, oh, tell me, say you will pity me! that you will pity me! that you will not throw me from you like a poisoned thing!

GEORGE. Zoe, explain yourself—your language fills me with shapeless fears.

ZOE. And what shall I say? I—my mother was—no, no—not her! Why should I refer the blame to her? George, do you see that hand you hold; look at these fingers, do you see the nails are of a blueish tinge?

GEORGE. Yes, near the quick there is a faint blue mark.

ZOE. Look in my eyes; is not the same color in the white?

GEORGE. It is their beauty.

ZOE. Could you see the roots of my hair you would see the same dark fatal mark. Do you know what that is?

GEORGE. No.

ZOE. That—that is the ineffacable curse of Cain.[1] Of the blood that feeds my heart, one drop in eight is black—bright red as the rest may be, that one drop poisons all the blood. Those seven bright drops give me love like yours, hope like yours—ambition like yours—life hung with passions like dew-drops on the morning flowers; but the one black drop gives me despair, for I'm an unclean thing—forbidden by the laws[2]—I'm an Octoroon!

GEORGE. Zoe, I love you none the less; this knowledge brings no revolt to my heart, and I can overcome the obstacle.

ZOE. But *I* cannot.

GEORGE. We can leave this country and go far away where none can know.

ZOE. And our mother, she, who from infancy treated me with such fondness, she who, as you said, had most reason to spurn me, can she forget what I am? Will she gladly see you wedded to the child of her husband's slave? No! she would revolt from it, as all but you would; and if I consented to hear the cries of my heart, if I did not crush out my infant love, what would she say to the poor girl on whom she had bestowed so much? No, no!

GEORGE. Zoe, must we immolate our lives on her prejudice?

ZOE. Yes, for I'd rather be black than ungrateful! Ah, George, our race has at least one virtue—it knows how to suffer.

GEORGE. Each word you utter makes my love sink deeper into my heart.

ZOE. And I remained here to induce you to offer that heart to Dora!

GEORGE. If you bid me do so I will obey you—

---

1   *curse of Cain* Cf. Genesis 4.11-15; after Cain, the son of Adam and Eve, killed his brother Abel, God said to him: "[Y]ou are cursed from the ground, which has opened its mouth to receive your brother's blood from your hand. ... And the LORD put a mark on Cain, lest any who came upon him should kill him." In the nineteenth century some people held the fallacious belief that God made the cursed man's skin black to mark him.

2   *forbidden by the laws* Louisiana law forbade miscegenation (the mixing of races).

ZOE. No, no! if you cannot be mine, oh, let me not blush when I think of you.

GEORGE. Dearest Zoe!

(*Exeunt. As they exit* M'CLOSKY *rises from behind rock, and looks after them.*)

M'CLOSKY. She loves him! I felt it—and how she can love! (*Advances.*) That one drop of black blood burns in her veins, and lights up her heart like a foggy sun. Oh, how I lapped up her words like a thirsty bloodhound! I'll have her if it costs me my life! Yonder the boy still lurks with those mailbags; the devil still keeps him here to tempt me, darn his yellow skin—I arrived just too late, he had grabbed the prize as I came up. Hillo! he's coming this way, fighting with his Ingiun. (*Conceals himself.*)

(*Enter* PAUL, *wrestling with* WAHNOTEE.)

PAUL. It ain't no use now, you got to gib it up!

WAHNOTEE. Ugh!

PAUL. It won't do! you got dat bottle of rum hid under your blanket—gib it up now, you—Yar! (*Wrenches it from him.*) You nasty, lying, Ingiun! It no use you putting on airs; I ain't gwine to sit up wid you all night, and you drunk. Hillo! war's the crowd gone? And dar's de 'paratus—oh gosh! if I could take a likeness of dis child! Uh, uh, let's have a peep. (*Looks through camera.*) Oh, golly! yah, you Wahnotee! you stan' dah,[1] I see you. Ta demine usti.[2] (*Looks at* WAHNOTEE *through the camera;* WAHNOTEE *springs back with an expression of alarm.*)

WAHNOTEE. No tue Wahnotee.[3]

PAUL. Ha, ha! tinks it's a gun; you ign'ant Ingiun, it can't hurt you! Stop, here's dem dishes—plates—dat's what he call 'em, all fix; I see Mas'r Scudder do it often—tink I can take likeness—stay dere, Wahnotee.

---

1 *you stan' dah* You stand there.

2 *Ta demine usti* Translation of the previous words into the "mashup" of languages understood by Wahnotee. There are several similar instances in which the "mashup" language is used, and translated either before or afterwards by Paul.

3 *No tue Wahnotee* Don't kill Wahnotee.

WAHNOTEE. No, carabine tue.

PAUL. I must operate and take my own likeness too—how debbel I do dat? Can't be ober dar an' here too—I ain't twins. Ugh! ach! 'Top, you look, you Wahnotee, you see dis rag, eh? Well, when I say go, den lift dis rag like dis, see! den run to dat pine tree up dar (*Points.*), and back agin, and den pull down de rag, so, d'ye see?

WAHNOTEE. Hugh!

PAUL. Den you hab glass ob rum.

WAHNOTEE. Rum!

PAUL. Dat wakes him up. Coute Wahnotee in Omenee dit, go, Wahnotee, poina la fa, comb a pine tree, la revient sala, la fa.

WAHNOTEE. Firewater!

PAUL. Yes, den a glass ob fire water, now den. (*Throws mailbags down, and sits on them.*) Pret, now den, go.

(WAHNOTEE *raises apron, and runs off.* PAUL *sits for his picture—* M'CLOSKY *appears.*)

M'CLOSKY. Where are they? Ah, yonder goes the Indian!

PAUL. De time he gone just about enough to cook dat dish plate.

M'CLOSKY. Yonder is the boy—now is my time! What's he doing? Is he asleep? (*Advances.*) He is sitting on my prize! Darn his carcase! I'll clear him off there—he'll never know what stunned him. (*Takes* WAHNOTEE'*s tomahawk and steals to* PAUL.)

PAUL. Dam dat Injun! is dat him creeping dar? I daren't move fear to spile myself.

(M'CLOSKY *strikes him on the head; he falls dead.*)

M'CLOSKY. Hooraw! the bags are mine—now for it! (*Opens mail-bags.*) What's here? Sunnyside, Pointdexter, Jackson, Peyton; here it is—the Liverpool postmark, sure enough! (*Opens letter—reads.*) "Madam, we are instructed by the firm of Mason and Co. to inform you that a dividend of forty per cent is payable on the 1st proximo,[1] this amount in consideration of position, they send herewith, and you will

---

1 *proximo* Next or coming month.

find enclosed by draft to your order on the bank of Louisiana, which please acknowledge—the balance will be paid in full, with interest, in three, six, and nine months—your drafts on Mason Brothers, at those dates, will be accepted by La Pelisse and Compagnie, N.O., so that you may command immediate use of the whole amount at once if required. Yours, &c, James Brown." What a find! this infernal letter would have saved all. (*During the reading of letter he remains nearly motionless under the focus of camera.*) But now I guess it will arrive too late— these darned U.S. mails are to blame. The Injun! he must not see me. (*Exit rapidly.*)

(WAHNOTEE *runs on, pulls down apron—sees* PAUL *lying on ground—speaks to him—thinks he is shamming sleep—gesticulates and jabbers—goes to him, moves him with feet, then kneels down to rouse him—to his horror finds him dead—expresses great grief—raises his eyes—they fall upon the camera—rises with savage growl, seizes tomahawk, and smashes camera to pieces, then goes to* PAUL—*expresses grief, sorrow, and fondness, and takes him in his arms to carry him away—Tableau.[1]*)

ACT 3

(*A Room in* MRS. PEYTON'S *house. An auction bill stuck up.* SOLON *and* GRACE *discovered.*)

PETE. (*Outside.*) Dis way—dis way.

(*Enter* PETE, POINTDEXTER, JACKSON, LAFOUCHE, *and* CAILLOU.)

PETE. Dis way, gen'lmen; now Solon—Grace—dey's hot and tirsty—sangaree,[2] brandy, rum.
JACKSON. Well, what d'ye say, Lafouche—d'ye smile?

---

1   *Tableau*   The device of the tableau, or a moment when all the actors freeze into a still picture to indicate a particularly significant point in the plot, was commonly used at the end of a scene or act in Victorian melodrama.
2   *sangaree*   From the Spanish "sangria," a sweet chilled drink made with wine and fruit juice.

(*Enter* THIBODEAUX *and* SUNNYSIDE.)

THIB. I hope we don't intrude on the family.

PETE. You see dat hole in dar, sar? (*Pointing to door.*) I was raised on dis yar plantation—neber see no door in it—always open, sar, for stranger to walk in.

SUNNYSIDE. And for substance to walk out.

(*Enter* RATTS.)

RATTS. Fine southern style that, eh?

LAFOUCHE. (*Reading bill.*) "A fine, well-built old family mansion, replete with every comfort."

RATTS. There's one name on the list of slaves scratched, I see.

LAFOUCHE. Yes; No. 49, Paul, a quadroon boy, aged thirteen.

SUNNYSIDE. He's missing.

POINT. Run away, I suppose.

PETE. (*Indignantly.*) No, sar; nigger nebber cut stick on Terrebonne; dat boy's dead, sure.

RATTS. What, Picayune Paul, as we called him, that used to come aboard my boat?—poor little darkey, I hope not; many a picayune he picked up for his dance and nigger songs, and he supplied our table with fish and game from the bayous.[1]

PETE. Nebber supply no more, sar—nebber dance again. Massa Ratts, you h'ard him sing about de place where de good niggers go de last time?

RATTS. Well?

PETE. Well, he gone dar hisself; why I tink so—'cause we missed Paul for some days, but nebber tout nothin', till one night dat ingiun Wahnotee suddenly stood right dare 'mongst us—was in his war paint, and mighty cold and grave—he sit down by de fire. "Whar's Paul?" I say—he smoke and smoke, but nebber look out ob de fire; well knowing dem critters, I wait a long time—den he say, "Wahnotee great chief"; den I say nothing—smoke anoder time—at last, rising to go, he turned round at door, and say berry low—oh, like a woman's voice— he say, "Omenee Pangeuk"—dat is, Paul is dead—nebber see him since.

---

1 *bayous* Swampy lake or river outlets, primarily in Louisiana and Mississippi.

RATTS. That redskin killed him.

SUNNYSIDE. So we believe; and so mad are the folks around, that if they catch the redskin they'll lynch him, sure.

RATTS. Lynch him! Darn his copper carcass, I've got a set of Irish deckhands aboard that just loved that child; and after I tell them this, let them get a sight of the redskin, I believe they would eat him, tomahawk and all. Poor little Paul!

THIB. What was he worth?

RATTS. Well, near on 500 dollars.

PETE. (*Scandalized.*) What, sar! You p'tend to be sorry for Paul, and prize him like dat—500 dollars! Tousand dollars, Massa Thibodeaux.

(*Enter* SCUDDER.)

SCUDDER. Gentlemen, the sale takes place at three. (*To* POINTDEXTER.) Good morning, Colonel. It's near that now, and there's still the sugar-houses to be inspected. Good day, Mr. Thibodeaux—shall we drive down that way? Mr. Lafouche, why, how do you do, sir? you're looking well.

LAFOUCHE. Sorry I can't return the compliment.

RATTS. Salem's looking kinder hollowed out.

SCUDDER. What Mr. Ratts, are you going to invest in swamps?

RATTS. No; I want a nigger.

SCUDDER. Hush.

PETE. Eh? wass dat?

SCUDDER. Mr. Sunnyside, I can't do this job of showin' round the folks; my stomach goes agin it. I want Pete here a minute.

SUNNYSIDE. I'll accompany them, certainly.

SCUDDER. (*Eagerly.*) Will ye? Thank ye! thank ye!

SUNNYSIDE. We must excuse Scudder, friends. I'll see you round the estate.

(*Enter* GEORGE *and* MRS. PEYTON.)

LAFOUCHE. Good morning, Mrs. Peyton. (*All salute.*)

SUNNYSIDE. This way, gentlemen.

RATTS. (*Aside to* SUNNYSIDE.) I say, I'd like to say summit soft to the old woman; perhaps it wouldn't go well, would it?

THIB. No; leave it alone.

RATTS. Darn it, when I see a woman in trouble, I feel like selling the skin off my back.

(*Exit* THIBODEAUX, SUNNYSIDE, RATTS, POINTDEXTER, GRACE, JACKSON, LAFOUCHE, CAILLOU, SOLON.)

SCUDDER. (*Aside to* PETE.) Go outside there; listen to what you hear, then go down to the quarters and tell the boys, for I can't do it. Oh, get out.

PETE. He said, I want a nigger; laws! mussey! what am going to cum ob us! (*Exit slowly, as if concealing himself.*)

GEORGE. My dear aunt, why do you not move from this painful scene? Go with Dora to Sunnyside.

MRS. P. No, George, your uncle said to me with his dying breath, "Nellie, never leave Terrebonne," and I never *will* leave it, till the law compels me.

SCUDDER. Mr. George—I'm going to say somethin' that has been chokin' me for some time. I know you'll excuse it—that's Miss Dora—that girl's in love with you; yes, sir, her eyes are startin' out of her head with it; now her fortune would redeem a good part of this estate.

MRS. P. Why, George, I never suspected this!

GEORGE. I did, aunt, I confess, but—

MRS. P. And you hesitated, from motives of delicacy?

SCUDDER. No, ma'am, here's the plan of it; Mr. George is in love with Zoe.

GEORGE. Scudder!

MRS. P. George!

SCUDDER. Hold on now! things have got so jammed in on top of us, we ain't got time to put kid gloves on to handle them. He loves Zoe, and has found out that she loves him. (*Sighing.*) Well, that's all right, but as he can't marry her, and as Miss Dora would jump at him—

MRS. P. Why didn't you mention this before?

SCUDDER. Why, because *I* love Zoe too, and I couldn't take that young feller from her, and she jist living on the sight of him, as I saw her do, and they so happy in spite of this yere misery around them, and they reproachin' themselves with not feeling as they ought. I've seen it, I tell you, and darn it, ma'am, can't you see that's what's been a hollowing me out so—I beg your pardon.

MRS. P. Oh, George—my son, let me call you—I do not speak for my own sake, nor for the loss of the estate, but for the poor people here; they will be sold, divided, and taken away—they have been born here. Heaven has denied me children, so all the strings of my heart have grown around and amongst them like the fibres and roots of an old tree in its native earth. Oh, let all go, but save them! with them around us, if we have not wealth, we shall at least have the home that they alone can make—

GEORGE. My dear mother—Mr. Scudder—you teach me what I ought to do; if Miss Sunnyside will accept me as I am, Terrebonne shall be saved; I will sell myself, but the slaves shall be protected.

MRS. P. *Sell* yourself, George! is not Dora worth any man's—

SCUDDER. Don't say that, ma'am; don't say that to a man that loves another gal; he's going to do a heroic act, don't spile it.

MRS. P. But Zoe is only an Octoroon!

SCUDDER. She's won this race agin the white anyhow; it's too late now to start her pedigree. (*As* DORA *enters.*) Come, Mrs. Peyton, take my arm; hush! here's the other one; she is a little too thoroughbred—too much of the greyhound, but the heart's there, I believe. (*Exit with* MRS. PEYTON.)

DORA. Poor Mrs. Peyton.

GEORGE. Miss Sunnyside, permit me a word; a feeling of delicacy has suspended on my lips an avowal, which—

DORA. (*Aside.*) Oh dear, has he suddenly come to his senses?

(*Enter* ZOE. *She stops at back.*)

GEORGE. In a word—I have seen and admired you!

DORA. (*Aside.*) He has a strange way of showing it—European, I suppose.

GEORGE. If you would pardon the abruptness of the question, I would ask you—Do you think the sincere devotion of my life to make yours happy would succeed?

DORA. (*Aside.*) Well, he has the oddest way of making love.

GEORGE. You are silent?

DORA. Mr. Peyton, I presume you have hesitated to make this avowal, because you feared in the present condition of affairs here, your object might be misconstrued, and that your attention was rather to my fortune than myself. (*A pause.*) Why don't he speak?—I mean, you feared I might not give you credit for sincere and pure feelings. Well, you wrong me. I don't think you capable of anything else than—

GEORGE. No, I hesitated because an attachment I had formed before I had the pleasure of seeing you had not altogether died out.

DORA. (*Smiling.*) Some of those sirens of Paris, I presume. (*Pause.*) I shall endeavor not to be jealous of the past; perhaps I have no right to be. (*Pause.*) But now that vagrant love is—eh, faded—is it not? Why don't you speak, sir?

GEORGE. Because, Miss Sunnyside, I have not learned to lie.

DORA. Good gracious—who wants you to?

GEORGE. I do, but I can't do it. No, the love I speak of is not such as you suppose—it is a passion that has grown up here, since I arrived; but it is a hopeless, mad, wild feeling, that must perish.

DORA. Here! since you arrived! Impossible; you have seen no one; whom can you mean?

ZOE. (*Advancing.*) Me.

GEORGE. Zoe!

DORA. You!

ZOE. Forgive him, Dora, for he knew no better until I told him. Dora, you are right; he is incapable of any but sincere and pure feelings—so are you. He loves me—what of that? you know you can't be jealous of a poor creature like me. If he caught the fever, were stung by a snake, or possessed of any other poisonous or unclean thing, you could pity, tend, love him through it, and for your gentle care he would love you in return. Well, is he not thus afflicted now? I am his love—he loves an Octoroon.

GEORGE. Oh, Zoe, you break my heart!

DORA. At college they said I was a fool—I must be. At New Orleans they said, "She's pretty, very pretty, but no brains."

I'm afraid they must be right; I can't understand a word of all this.

ZOE. Dear Dora, try to understand it with your heart. You love George, you love him dearly, I know it, and you deserve to be loved by him. He will love you—he must; his love for me will pass away—it shall. You heard him say it was hopeless. Oh, forgive him and me!

DORA. (*Weeping.*) Oh, why did he speak to me at all, then? You've made me cry, then, and I hate you both! (*Exit through room.*)

(*Enter* MRS. PEYTON *and* SCUDDER, M'CLOSKY *and* POINTDEXTER.)

M'CLOSKY. I'm sorry to intrude, but the business I came upon will excuse me.

MRS. P. Here is my nephew, sir.

ZOE. Perhaps I had better go.

M'CLOSKY. Wal, as it consarns[1] you, perhaps you better had.

SCUDDER. Consarns Zoe?

M'CLOSKY. I don't know, she may as well hear the hull of it. Go on, Colonel Pointdexter. Ma'am—the mortgagee, auctioneer, and general agent.

POINT. Pardon me, madam, but do you know these papers? (*Hands papers to* MRS. PEYTON.)

MRS. P. (*Taking them.*) Yes, sir, they were the free-papers of the girl Zoe; but they were in my husband's secretaire—how came they in your possession?

M'CLOSKY. I—I found them.

GEORGE. And you purloined them?

M'CLOSKY. Hold on, you'll see. Go on, Colonel.

POINT. The list of your slaves is incomplete—it wants one.

SCUDDER. The boy Paul—we know it.

POINT. No sir, you have omitted the Octoroon girl, Zoe.

MRS. P. Zoe!

ZOE. Me!

POINT. At the time the judge executed those free-papers to his

---

1 *consarns* Concerns.

infant slave, a judgment stood recorded against him; while that was on record he had no right to make away with his property. That judgment still exists—under it and others this estate is sold today. Those free-papers ain't worth the sand that's on 'em.

MRS. P. Zoe a slave! It is impossible!

POINT. It is certain, madam; the judge was negligent, and, doubtless, forgot this small formality.

SCUDDER. But the creditors will not claim the gal?

M'CLOSKY. Excuse me; one of the principal mortgagees has made the demand. (*Exit with* POINTDEXTER.)

SCUDDER. Hold on yere, George Peyton, you sit down there; you're trembling so, you'll fall down directly—this blow has staggered me some.

MRS. P. Oh, Zoe, my child! don't think too hardly of your poor father.

ZOE. I shall do so if you weep—see, I'm calm.

SCUDDER. Calm as a tombstone, and with about as much life—I see it in your face.

GEORGE. It cannot be! It shall not be!

SCUDDER. Hold your tongue—it must; be calm—darn the things! the proceeds of this sale won't cover the debts of the estate. Consarn[1] those Liverpool English fellers, why couldn't they send something by the last mail? Even a letter promising something—such is the feeling round amongst the planters—darn me if I couldn't raise thirty thousand on the envelope alone, and ten thousand more on the postmark.

GEORGE. Zoe, they shall not take you from us while I live.

SCUDDER. Don't be a fool; they'd kill you, and then take her, just as soon as—stop, old Sunnyside, he'll buy her! that'll save her.

ZOE. No, it won't; we have confessed to Dora that we love each other. How can she then ask her father to free me?

SCUDDER. What in thunder made you do that?

ZOE. Because it was the truth, and I had rather be a slave with a free soul than remain free with a slavish, deceitful heart.

---

1   *Consarn*   Here, the word is used in the sense of "confound."

My father gives me freedom—at least he thought so—may heaven bless him for the thought, bless him for the happiness he spread around my life. You say the proceeds of the sale will not cover his debts—let me be sold then, that I may free his name—I give him back the liberty he bestowed upon me, for I can never repay him the love he bore his poor Octoroon child, on whose breast his last sigh was drawn, into whose eyes he looked with the last gaze of affection.

MRS. P. Oh! my husband! I thank heaven you have not lived to see this day.

ZOE. George, leave me. I would be alone a little while.

GEORGE. Zoe! (*Turns away overpowered.*)

ZOE. Do not weep, George—dear George, you now see what a miserable thing I am.

GEORGE. Zoe!

SCUDDER. I wish they could sell *me*! I brought half this ruin on this family, with my all-fired improvements; I deserve to be a nigger this day—I feel like one inside. (*Exit.*)

ZOE. Go now, George—leave me—take her with you. (*Exit* MRS. PEYTON *and* GEORGE.) A slave! a slave! Is this a dream—for my brain reels with the blow? He said so. What! then I shall be sold!—sold! and my master—oh! (*Falls on her knees with her face in her hands.*) No—no master but one. George—George! Hush, they come! save me! No, (*Looks off.*) 'tis Pete and the servants—they come this way. (*Enters inner room.*)

(*Enter* PETE, GRACE, MINNIE, SOLON, DIDO, *and all Negroes.*)

PETE. Cum yer now—stand round, 'cause I've got to talk to you darkies—keep dem children quiet—don't make no noise, de missus up dar har us.

SOLON. Go on, Pete.

PETE. Gen'l'men, my colored frens and ladies, dar's mighty bad news gone round. Dis yer prop'ty to be sold—old Terrebonne whar we all been raised, is gwine—dey's gwine to take it away—can't stop here no how..

OMNES.[1] Oo!—Oo!

---

1 OMNES Latin: All, or everyone.

PETE. Hold quiet, you trash o' niggers! tink anybody wants you to cry? Who's you to set up screeching?—be quiet! But dis ain't all. Now, my culled brethren, gird up your lines, and listen—hold on your bret—it's a-comin'—we taught dat de niggers would belong to de old missus, and if she lost Terrebonne, we must live dere allers, and we would hire out, and bring our wages to ole Missus Peyton.

OMNES. Ya! ha! Well—

PETE. Hush! I tell ye, taint so—we can't do it—we've got to be sold—

OMNES. Sold!

PETE. Will you hush? she will hear you. Yes! I listen dar jess now—dar was ole lady cryin'—Massa George—ah! you seen dem big tears in his eyes. Oh, Massa Scudder, he didn't cry zackly;[1] both ob his eye and cheek look like de bad bayou in low season—so dry dat I cry for him. (*Raising his voice.*) Den say de missus, "Taint for de land I keer, but for dem poor niggers—dey'll be sold—dat wot stagger me." "No," say Massa George, "I'd rather sell myself fuss; but they shan't suffer no how—I see 'em dam fuss."

OMNES. Oh, bless urn! Bless Mas'r George.

PETE. Hole yer tongues. Yes, for you, for me, for dem little ones, dem folks cried. Now den, if Grace dere wid her chil'n were all sold, she'll begin screetchin' like a cat. She didn't mind how kind old judge was to her; and Solon, too, he'll holler, and break de ole lady's heart.

GRACE. No, Pete; no, I won't. I'll bear it.

PETE. I don't tink you will any more, but dis here will, 'cause de family spile Dido, day has. She nebber was worth much 'a dat nigger.

DIDO. How dar you say dat? you black nigger, you. I fetch as much as any odder cook in Louisiana.

PETE. What's de use of your takin' it kind, and comfortin' de missus heart, if Minnie dere, and Louise, and Marie, and Julia is to spile it?

MINNIE. We won't, Pete; we won't.

---

1 *zackly* Exactly.

PETE. (*To the men.*) Dar, do ye hear dat, ye mis'able darkeys; dem gals is worth a boatload of kinder men, dem is. Cum, for de pride of de family, let every darkey look his best for de judge's sake—dat ole man so good to us, and dat ole woman—so dem strangers from New Orleans shall say, dem's happy darkies, dem's a fine set of niggers; every one say when he's sold, "Lor' bless dis yer family I'm gwine out of and send me as good a home."

OMNES. We'll do it, Pete; we'll do it.

PETE. Hush! hark! I tell ye dar's somebody in dar. Who is it?

GRACE. It's Missy Zoe. See! see!

PETE. Come along; she har what we say, and she's crying 'fore us. None o' ye ig'rant niggers could cry for yerselves like dat. Come here quite; now quite. (*Exit* PETE *and all the Negroes, slowly.*)

(*Enter* ZOE, *supposed to have overheard the last scene.*)

ZOE. Oh! must I learn from these poor wretches how much I owe, and how I ought to pay the debt? Have I slept upon the benefits I received, and never saw, never felt, never knew that I was forgetful and ungrateful? Oh, my father! my dear, dear father! forgive your poor child; you made her life too happy, and now these tears will flow; let me hide them till I teach my heart. Oh, my—my heart! (*Exit with a low wailing suffocating cry.*)

(*Enter* M'CLOSKY, LAFOUCHE, JACKSON, SUNNYSIDE *and* POINT-DEXTER.)

POINT. (*Looking at watch.*) Come, the hour is past. I think we may begin business. Where is Mr. Scudder?

JACKSON. I want to get to Ophelensis tonight.

(*Enter* DORA.)

DORA. Father, come here.

SUNNYSIDE. Why, Dora, what's the matter? your eyes are red.

DORA. Are they? thank you. I don't care, they were blue this morning, but it don't signify now.

SUNNYSIDE. My darling! who has been teasing you?

Dora. Never mind. I want you to buy Terrebonne.

Sunnyside. Buy Terrebonne! What for?

Dora. No matter—buy it!

Sunnyside. It will cost me all I'm worth—this is folly, Dora.

Dora. Is my plantation at Comptableau worth this?

Sunnyside. Nearly—perhaps.

Dora. Sell it, then, and buy this.

Sunnyside. Are you mad, my love?

Dora. Do you want *me* to stop here and *bid* for it?

Sunnyside. Good gracious! no.

Dora. Then I'll do it, if you don't.

Sunnyside. I will! I will! But for heaven's sake go—here comes the crowd. (*Exit* Dora.) What on earth does that child mean or want?

(*Enter* Scudder, George, Ratts, Caillou, Pete, Grace, Minnie *and all the negroes. A large table is in the centre at back.* Pointdexter *mounts the table with his hammer—his* Clerk *sits at his feet. A* Negro *mounts the table from behind. The company sit.*)

Point. Now, gentlemen, we shall proceed to business. It ain't necessary for me to dilate, describe, or enumerate; Terrebonne is known to you as one of the richest bits of sile[1] in Louisiana, and its condition reflects credit on them as had to keep it. I'll trouble you for that piece of baccy,[2] Judge—thank you—so, gentlemen, as life is short, we'll start right off. The first lot on here is the estate in block, with its sugar houses, stock machines, implements, good dwelling houses and furniture; if there is no bid for the estate and stuff we'll sell it in smaller lots. Come, Mr. Thibodeaux, a man has a chance once in his life—here's yours.

Thib. Go on. What's the reserve bid?

Point. The first mortgagee bids forty thousand dollars.

Thib. Forty-five thousand.

Sunnyside. Fifty thousand.

---

1   *sile*   Soil.
2   *baccy*   Chewing tobacco.

POINT. When you have done joking, gentlemen, you'll say one hundred and twenty thousand; it carried that easy on mortgage.

LAFOUCHE. Then why don't you buy it yourself, Colonel?

POINT. I'm waiting on your fifty thousand bid.

CAILLOU. Eighty thousand.

POINT. Don't be afraid, it ain't going for that, Judge.

SUNNYSIDE. Ninety thousand.

POINT. We're getting on.

THIB. One hundred—

POINT. One hundred thousand bid for this mag—

CAILLOU. One hundred and ten thousand—

POINT. Good again—one hundred and—

SUNNYSIDE. Twenty.

POINT. And twenty thousand bid. Squire Sunnyside is going to sell this at fifty thousand advance tomorrow. (*Looks round.*) Where's that man from Mobile that wanted to give one hundred and eighty thousand?

THIB. I guess he ain't left home yet, Colonel.

POINT. I shall knock it down to the Squire—going—gone—for 120,000 dollars. (*Raises hammer.*) Judge, you can raise the hull on mortgage—going for half its value. (*Knocks.*) Squire Sunnyside, you've got a pretty bit o' land, squire. Hillo, darkey, hand me a smash[1] dar.

SUNNYSIDE. I got more than I can work now.

POINT. Then buy the hands along with the property. Now, gentlemen, I'm proud to submit to you the finest lot of field hands and house servants that were ever offered for competition; they speak for themselves, and do credit to their owners. (*Reads.*) "No. 1, Solon, a guest boy and good waiter."

PETE. That's my son—buy him, Mass'r Ratts, he's sure to serve you well.

POINT. Hold your tongue!

RATTS. Let the darkey alone—800 for that boy.

CAILLOU. Nine.

---

1 *smash* Drink made from mint, soda, sugar, and brandy or other liquor.

RATTS. A thousand.

SOLON. Thank you, Massa Ratts, I die for you, sar; hold up for me, sar.

RATTS. Look here, the boy knows and likes me, Judge; let him come my way.

CAILLOU. Go on, I'm dumb.

POINT. One thousand bid. (*Knocks.*) He's yours, Captain Ratts, Magnolia steamer.

(SOLON *goes and stands behind* RATTS.) "No. 2, the yellow girl, Grace, with two children—Saul, aged 4, and Victoria, 5." (*They get on table.*)

SCUDDER. That's Solon's wife and children, Judge.

GRACE. (*To* RATTS.) Buy me, Massa Ratts, do buy me, sar.

RATTS. What in thunder should I do with you and those devils on board my boat.

GRACE. Wash, sar—cook, sar—anything.

RATTS. Eight hundred agin, then—I'll go it.

JACKSON. Nine.

RATTS. I'm broke, Solon—I can't stop the judge.

THIB. What's the matter, Ratts? I'll lend you all you want. Go in, if you've a mind to.

RATTS. Eleven.

JACKSON. Twelve.

SUNNYSIDE. Oh, oh!

SCUDDER. (*To* JACKSON.) Judge, my friend. The judge is a little deaf. Hello! (*Speaking in his ear-trumpet.*) This gal and them children belong to that boy Solon there. You're bidding to separate them, Judge.

JACKSON. The devil I am! (*Rises.*) I'll take back my bid, Colonel.

POINT. All right, Judge; I thought there was a mistake. I must keep you, Captain, to the eleven hundred.

RATTS. Go it.

POINT. Eleven hundred—going—going—sold! "No. 3, Pete, a house-servant."

PETE. Dat's me—yer, I'm comin'—stand around dar. (*Tumbles upon the table.*)

POINT. Aged seventy-two.

PETE. What's dat? a mistake, sar—forty-six.

POINT. Lame.

PETE. But don't mount to nuffin—kin work cannel.[1] Come, Judge! pick up—now's your time, sar.

JACKSON. One hundred dollars.

PETE. What, sar? me! for me—look ye here. (*Dances.*)

GEORGE. Five hundred.

PETE. Massa George—ah no, sar—don't buy me—keep your money for some udder dat is to be sold. I ain't no count, sar.

POINT. Five hundred bid—it's a good price. (*Knocks.*) He's yours, Mr. George Peyton. (PETE *goes down.*) "No. 4, the Octoroon girl, Zoe."

(*Enter* ZOE, *very pale, and stands on table—hitherto* M'CLOSKY *has taken no interest in the sale, now turns his chair.*)

SUNNYSIDE. (*Rising.*) Gentlemen, we are all acquainted with the circumstances of this girl's position, and I feel sure that no one here will oppose the family who desires to redeem the child of our esteemed and noble friend, the late Judge Peyton.

OMNES. Hear! bravo! hear!

POINT. While the proceeds of this sale promises to realize less than the debts upon it, it is my duty to prevent any collusion for the depreciation of the property.

RATTS. Darn ye! you're a man as well as an auctioneer, ain't ye?

POINT. What is offered for this slave?

SUNNYSIDE. One thousand dollars.

M'CLOSKY. Two thousand.

SUNNYSIDE. Three thousand.

M'CLOSKY. Five thousand.

GEORGE. Demon!

SUNNYSIDE. I bid seven thousand, which is the last dollar this family possesses.

M'CLOSKY. Eight.

THIB. Nine.

OMNES. Bravo!

M'CLOSKY. Ten. It's no use, Squire.

---

1   *cannel*   Alternative spelling of cannelle, or cinnamon.

SCUDDER. Jacob M'Closky, you shan't have that girl. Now, take care what you do. Twelve thousand.

M'CLOSKY. Shan't I? Fifteen thousand. Beat that any of ye.

POINT. Fifteen thousand bid for the Octoroon.

(*Enter* DORA.)

DORA. Twenty thousand.

OMNES. Bravo!

M'CLOSKY. Twenty-five thousand.

OMNES. (*Groan.*) Oh! oh!

GEORGE. Yelping hound—take that! (*Rushes on* M'CLOSKY, *who draws his knife.*)

SCUDDER. (*Darting between them.*) Hold on, George Peyton— stand back. This is your own house; we are under your uncle's roof; recollect yourself. And, strangers, ain't we forgittin' there's a lady present. (*The knives disappear.*) If we can't behave like Christians, let's try and act like gentlemen. Go on, Colonel.

LAFOUCHE. He didn't ought to bid against a lady.

M'CLOSKY. Oh, that's it, is it? then I'd like to hire a lady to go to auction to buy my hands.

POINT. Gentlemen, I believe none of us have two feelings about the conduct of that man; but he has the law on his side—we may regret, but we must respect it. Mr. M'Closky has bid twenty-five thousand dollars for the Octoroon. Is there any other bid? For the first time, twenty-five thousand—last time! (*Brings hammer down.*) To Jacob M'Closky, the Octoroon girl Zoe, twenty-five thousand dollars.

(*Tableau.*)[1]

---

1 *Tableau* This is the tableau that is illustrated on the cover of this edition.

Act 4

(The Wharf. The Steamer "Magnolia" alongside. A bluff rock upstage right. RATTS discovered, supervising the loading of ship. Enter LAFOUCHE and JACKSON.)

JACKSON. How long before we start, captain?

RATTS. Just as soon as we put this cotton on board.

(Enter PETE, with lantern, and SCUDDER, with notebook.)

SCUDDER. One hundred and forty-nine bales. Can you take any more?

RATTS. Not a bale. I've got engaged eight hundred bales at the next landing, and one hundred hogsheads of sugar at Patten's Slide—that'll take my guards under—hurry up thar!

VOICE. *(Outside.)* Wood's aboard.

RATTS. All aboard then.

(Enter M'CLOSKY.)

SCUDDER. Sign the receipt, captain, and save me going up to the clerk.

M'CLOSKY. See here—there's a small freight of turpentine in the forehold there, and one of the barrels leaks; a spark from your engines might set the ship on fire, and you'd go with it.

RATTS. You be darned! Go and try it if you've a mind to.

LAFOUCHE. Captain, you've loaded up here until the boat is sunk so deep in the mud she won't float.

RATTS. *(Calling off.)* Wood up thar, you Pollo—hang on to the safety valve—guess she'll crawl off on her paddles.

(Shouts heard.)

JACKSON. What's the matter?

(Enter SOLON.)

SOLON. We got him!

SCUDDER. Who?

SOLON. The Inginn!

SCUDDER. Wahnotee? where is he? d'ye call running away from a fellow catching him?

RATTS. Here he comes.

OMNES. Where? where?

(*Enter* WAHNOTEE; *they are all about to rush on him.*)

SCUDDER. Hold on! stan' round thar! no violence—the critter don't know what we mean.

JACKSON. Let him answer for the boy, then.

M'CLOSKY. Down with him—lynch him.

OMNES. Lynch him!

(*Exit* LAFOUCHE.)

SCUDDER. Stan' back, I say! I'll nip the first that lays a finger on him. Pete, speak to the redskin.

PETE. Whar's Paul, Wahnotee? What's come ob de child?

WAHNOTEE. Paul wunce—Paul pangeuk.

PETE. Pangeuk—dead.

WAHNOTEE. Mort!

M'CLOSKY. And you killed him?

(*They approach again.*)

SCUDDER. Hold on!

PETE. Um, Paul reste?

WAHNOTEE. Hugh vieu—(*Going left.*) Paul reste ci!

SCUDDER. Here, stay! (*Examines the ground.*) The earth has been stirred here lately.

WAHNOTEE. Weenee Paul. (*Points down and shows by pantomime how he buried* PAUL.)

SCUDDER. The Inginn means that he buried him there! Stop, here's a bit of leather. (*Draws out mail-bags.*) The mailbags that were lost! (*Sees tomahawk in* WAHNOTEE's *belt—draws it out and examines it.*) Look! here are marks of blood—look thar, redskin, what's that?

WAHNOTEE. Paul! (*Makes sign that* PAUL *was killed by a blow on the head.*)

M'CLOSKY. He confesses it; the Indian got drunk, quarrelled with him, and killed him.

(*Re-enter* LAFOUCHE, *with smashed apparatus.*)

LAFOUCHE. Here are evidences of the crime, this rum bottle half emptied—this photographic apparatus smashed—and there are marks of blood and footsteps around the shed.

M'CLOSKY. What more d'ye want—ain't that proof enough? Lynch him!

OMNES. Lynch him! Lynch him!

SCUDDER. Stan' back, boys! he's an Inginn—fair play.

JACKSON. Try him, then—try him on the spot of his crime.

OMNES. Try him! try him!

LAFOUCHE. Don't let him escape!

RATTS. I'll see to that. (*Draws revolver.*) If he stirs, I'll put a bullet through his skull, mighty quick.

M'CLOSKY. Come—form a court, then; choose a jury—we'll fix this varmin.

(*Enter* THIBODEAUX *and* CAILLOU.)

THIB. What's the matter?

LAFOUCHE. We've caught this murdering Inginn, and are going to try him.

(WAHNOTEE *sits, rolled in blanket.*)

PETE. Poor little Paul—poor little nigger!

SCUDDER. This business goes agin me, Ratts—'taint right.

LAFOUCHE. We're ready; the jury empanelled—go ahead—who'll be accuser?

RATTS. M'Closky.

M'CLOSKY. Me!

RATTS. Yes; you was the first to hail Judge Lynch.

M'CLOSKY. Well, what's the use of argument, whar guilt sticks out so plain? The boy and Inginn were alone when last seen.

SCUDDER. Who says that?

M'CLOSKY. Everybody—that is, I heard so.

SCUDDER. Say what you know—not what you heard.

M'CLOSKY. I know, then, that the boy was killed with that tomahawk—the redskin owns it—the signs of violence are all round the shed—this apparatus smashed—ain't it plain that in a drunken fit he slew the boy, and when sober concealed the body yonder?

OMNES. That's it—that's it.

RATTS. Who defends the Indian?

SCUDDER. I will; for it's agin my natur' to b'lieve him guilty; and if he be, this ain't the place, nor you the authority to try him. How are we sure the boy is dead at all? There are no witnesses but a rum bottle and an old machine. Is it on such evidence you'd hang a human being?

RATTS. His own confession.

SCUDDER. I appeal against your usurped authority; this Lynch law is a wild and lawless proceeding. Here's a pictur' for a civilized community to afford; yonder, a poor ignorant savage, and round him a circle of hearts, white with revenge and hate, thirsting for his blood; you call yourselves judges—you ain't—you're a jury of executioners. It is such scenes as these that bring disgrace upon our Western life.

M'CLOSKY. Evidence! Evidence! Give us evidence, we've had talk enough; now for proof.

OMNES. Yes, yes! Proof, proof!

SCUDDER. Where am I to get it? the proof is here, in my heart!

PETE. (*Who has been looking about the camera.*) "Top sar! 'top a bit! Oh, laws-a-mussey, see dis, here's a pictur' I found sticking in that yar telescope machine, sar! look, sar!

SCUDDER. A photographic plate. (PETE *holds lantern up.*) What's this, eh? two forms! the child—'tis he! dead—and above him—Ah! ah! Jacob M'Closky—'twas you murdered that boy!

M'CLOSKY. Me?

SCUDDER. You! You slew him with that tomahawk, and as you stood over his body with the letter in your hand, you thought that no witness saw the deed, that no eye was on you; but there was, Jacob M'Closky, there was—the eye of the Eternal was on you—the blessed sun in heaven, that, looking down, struck upon this plate the image of the deed. Here you are, in the very attitude of your crime!

M'CLOSKY. 'Tis false!

SCUDDER. 'Tis true! the apparatus can't lie. Look there, jurymen— (*Showing plate to jury.*)—look there. Oh, you wanted evidence—you called for proof—Heaven has answered and convicted you.

M'CLOSKY. What court of law would receive such evidence? (*Going.*)

RATTS. Stop! *this* would—you called it yourself; you wanted to make us murder that Inginn, and since we've got our hands in for justice, we'll try it on *you*. What say ye? shall we have one law for the redskin and another for the white?

OMNES. Try him! try him!

RATTS. Who'll be accuser?

SCUDDER. I will! Fellow citizens, you are convened and assembled here under a higher power than the law. What's the law? When the ship's abroad on the ocean—when the army is before the enemy—where in thunder's the law? It is in the hearts of brave men who can tell right from wrong, and from whom justice can't be bought. So it is here, in the wilds of the West, where our hatred of crime is measured by the speed of our executions—where necessity is law! I say, then, air you honest men? air you true? put your hands on your naked breasts, and let every man as don't feel a real American heart there, bustin' up with freedom, truth, and right, let that man step out. That's the oath I put to ye—and then say, darn ye, go it!

OMNES. Go on! Go on!

SCUDDER. No! I won't go on; that man's down—I won't strike him even with words. Jacob, your accuser is that picter of the crime—let that speak—defend yourself.

M'CLOSKY. (*Drawing knife.*) I will, quicker than lightning.

RATTS. Seize him, then! (*They rush on* M'CLOSKY *and disarm him.*) He can fight, though—he's a painter, claws all over.

SCUDDER. Stop! Search him; we may find more evidence.

M'CLOSKY. Would you rob me first, and murder me afterwards?

RATTS. (*Searching him.*) That's his programme—here's a pocketbook.

SCUDDER. (*Opening it.*) What's here? Letters! Hello! To "Mrs. Peyton, Terrebonne, Louisiana, United States." Liverpool postmark. Ho! I've got hold of the tail of a rat—come out. (*Reads.*) What's this?—a draft for 85,000 dollars, and credit on Palisse and Co., of New Orleans, for the balance. Hi! the rat's out—you killed the boy to steal this letter from the mailbag—

you stole this letter that the money should not arrive in time to save the Octoroon; had it done so, the lien on the estate would have ceased, and Zoe be free.

OMNES. Lynch him!—lynch him!—down with him!

SCUDDER. Silence in the court—stand back; let the gentlemen of the jury retire, consult, and return their verdict.

RATTS. I'm responsible for the crittur—go on.

PETE. (*To* WAHNOTEE.) See, Inginn, look far. (*Shows him plate.*) See dat innocent, look, dare's the murderer of poor Paul.

WAHNOTEE. Ugh! (*Examines plate.*)

PETE. Ya! as he? Closky tue[1] Paul—kill de child with your tomahawk dar; 'twasn't you, no—ole Pete allus say so. Poor Inginn lub[2] our little Paul.

(WAHNOTEE *rises and looks at* M'CLOSKY—*he is in his war paint and fully armed.*)

SCUDDER. What say ye, gentlemen? Is the prisoner guilty, or is he not guilty?

OMNES. Guilty!

SCUDDER. And what is to be his punishment?

OMNES. Death! (*All advance.*)

WAHNOTEE. (*Crossing to* M'CLOSKY.) Ugh!

SCUDDER. No, Inginn; we deal out justice here, not revenge. 'Tain't you he's injured, 'tis the white man, whose laws he has offended.

RATTS. Away with him—put him down the aft hatch, till we rig his funeral.

M'CLOSKY. Fifty against one! Oh, if I had you one by one alone in the swamp, I'd rip ye all. (*He is borne off in boat, struggling.*)

SCUDDER. Now, then, to business.

PETE. (*Re-entering from boat.*) O, law, sir, dat debil Closky, he tore hisself from de gen'lam, knock me down, take my light, and trows it on de turpentine barrels, and de shed's all afire! (*Fire seen.*)

JACKSON. (*Re-entering.*) We are catching fire forward; quick, cut free from the shore.

---

1 *tue* French: kill.
2 *lub* Love.

RATTS. All hands aboard there—cut the starn[1] ropes—give her headway!

ALL. Ay, ay!

(*Cry of "Fire" heard—engine bells heard—steam whistle noise.*)

RATTS. Cut all away forard—overboard with every bale afire.

(*The Steamer moves off—fire still blazing.* M'CLOSKY *re-enters, swimming.*)

M'CLOSKY. Ha! have I fixed ye? Burn! burn! that's right. You thought you had cornered me, did ye? As I swam down, I thought I heard something in the water, as if pursuing me—one of them darned alligators, I suppose—they swarm hereabout—may they crunch every limb of ye. (*Exit.*)

(WAHNOTEE *is seen swimming. He finds trail and follows* M'CLOSKY. *The Steamer floats on at back, burning.*)

ACT 5

SCENE 1. (*Negro Quarters. Enter* ZOE.)

ZOE. It wants an hour yet to daylight—here is Pete's hut— (*Knocks.*) He sleeps—no; I see a light.

DIDO. (*Entering from hut.*) Who dat?

ZOE. Hush, aunty! 'Tis I—Zoe.

DIDO. Missy Zoe! Why you out in de swamp dis time ob night; you catch de fever sure—you is all wet.

ZOE. Where's Pete?

DIDO. He gone down to de landing last night wid Mas'r Scudder; not come back since—kint[2] make it out.

ZOE. Aunty, there is sickness up at the house; I have been up all night beside one who suffers, and I remembered that when I had the fever you gave me a drink, a bitter drink that made me sleep—do you remember it?

---

1 *starn* Stern.
2 *kint* Can't.

DIDO. Didn't I? Dem doctors ain't no 'count; dey don't know nuffin.[1]

ZOE. No; but you, Aunty, you are wise—you know every plant, don't you, and what it is good for?

DIDO. Dat you drink is fust[2] rate for red fever. Is de folks' head bad?

ZOE. Very bad, Aunty; and the heart aches worse, so they can get no rest.

DIDO. Hold on a bit, I get you de bottle. (*Exit.*)

ZOE. In a few hours that man, my master, will come for me: he has paid my price, and he only consented to let me remain here this one night, because Mrs. Peyton promised to give me up to him today.

DIDO. (*Re-entering with phial.*) Here 'tis—now you give one timble-full—dat's nuff.[3]

ZOE. All there is there would kill one, wouldn't it?

DIDO. Guess it kill a dozen—nebber try.

ZOE. It's not a painful death, Aunty, is it? You told me it produced a long, long sleep.

DIDO. Why you tremble so? why you speak so wild? what you's gwine to do, missey?

ZOE. Give me the drink.

DIDO. No. Who dat sick at de house?

ZOE. Give it to me.

DIDO. No, you want to hurt yourself. Oh, Miss Zoe, why you ask old Dido for dis pizen?

ZOE. Listen to me. I love one who is here, and he loves me— George. I sat outside his door all night—I heard his sighs— his agony—torn from him by my coming fate; and he said, "I'd rather see her dead than his!"

DIDO. Dead!

ZOE. He said so—then I rose up, and stole from the house, and ran down to the bayou; but its cold, black, silent stream terrified me—drowning must be so horrible a death. I could not do it. Then, as I knelt there, weeping for courage, a snake

---

1 *nuffin* Nothing.
2 *fust* First.
3 *nuff* Enough.

rattled beside me. I shrunk from it and fled. Death was there beside me, and I dared not take it. Oh! I'm afraid to die; yet I am more afraid to live.

DIDO. Die!

ZOE. So I came here to you; to you, my own dear nurse; to you, who so often hushed me to sleep when I was a child; who dried my eyes and put your little Zoe to rest. Ah! give me the rest that no master but One can disturb—the sleep from which I shall awake free! You can protect me from that man— do let me die without pain.

DIDO. No, no—life is good for young ting like you.

ZOE. Oh! good, good nurse: you will, you will.

DIDO. No—g'way.

ZOE. Then I shall never leave Terrebonne—the drink, nurse; the drink; that I may never leave my home—my dear, dear home. You will not give me to that man? Your own Zoe, that loves you, Aunty, so much, so much. (*Gets phial.*) Ah! I have it.

DIDO. No, missey. Oh! no—don't.

ZOE. Hush! (*Runs off.*)

DIDO. Here, Solon, Minnie, Grace! (*They enter.*)

ALL. Was de matter?

DIDO Miss Zoe got de pizen. (*Exit.*)

ALL. Oh! oh! (*Exeunt.*)

SCENE 2. *Cane-brake Bayou: Bank, Triangle Fire—Canoe.*
M'CLOSKY *discovered asleep.*

M'CLOSKY. Burn, burn! blaze away! How the flames crack. I'm not guilty; would ye murder me? Cut, cut the rope—I choke—choke!—Ah! (*Wakes.*) Hello! where am I? Why, I was dreaming—curse it! I can never sleep now without dreaming. Hush! I thought I heard the sound of a paddle in the water. All night, as I fled through the cane-brake,[1] I heard footsteps behind me. I lost them in the cedar swamp—again they haunted my path down the bayou, moving as I moved, resting

---

1   *cane-brake*   Thicket of reeds.

when I rested—hush! there again!—no; it was only the wind over the canes. The sun is rising. I must launch my dugout, and put for the bay, and in a few hours I shall be safe from pursuit on board one of the coasting schooners that run from Galveston to Matagorda. In a little time this darned business will blow over, and I can show again! If it was the ghost of that murdered boy haunting me! Well—I didn't mean to kill him, did I? Well, then, what has my all-cowardly heart got to skeer me so for?

(*Gets in canoe and rows off.* WAHNOTEE *paddles canoe on, gets out and finds trail—paddles off after him.*)

SCENE 3. *Cedar swamp. Enter* SCUDDER *and* PETE.

SCUDDER. Come on, Pete, we shan't reach the house before midday.

PETE. Nebber mind, sa, we bring good news—it won't spile for de keeping.

SCUDDER. Ten miles we've had to walk, because some blamed varmin onhitched our dugout. I left it last night all safe.

PETE. P'r'aps it floated away itself.

SCUDDER. No; the hitching line was cut with a knife.

PETE. Say, Mas'r Scudder, s'pose we go in round by de quarters and raise de darkies, den dey cum long wid us, and we 'proach dat ole house like Gin'ral Jackson when he took London out dar.

SCUDDER. Hello, Pete, I never heard of that affair.

PETE. I tell you, sa—hush!

SCUDDER. What?

PETE. Was dat?—a cry out dar in the swamp—dar again!

SCUDDER. So it is. Something forcing its way through the undergrowth—it comes this way—it's either a bear or a runaway nigger. (*Draws pistol.* M'CLOSKY *rushes on and falls at* SCUDDER's *feet.*) Stand off—what are ye?

PETE. Mas'r Closky.

M'CLOSKY. Save me—save me! I can go no farther. I heard voices.

SCUDDER. Who's after you?

M'CLOSKY. I don't know, but I feel it's death! In some form, human, or wild beast, or ghost, it has tracked me through the night. I fled; it followed. Hark! there it comes—it comes—don't you hear a footstep on the dry leaves?

SCUDDER. Your crime has driven you mad.

M'CLOSKY. D'ye hear it—nearer—nearer—ah!

(WAHNOTEE *rushes on, and at* M'CLOSKY.)

SCUDDER. The Inginn! by thunder.

PETE. You'se a dead man, Mas'r Closky—you got to b'lieve dat.

M'CLOSKY. No—no. If I must die, give me up to the law; but save me from the tomahawk. You are a white man; you'll not leave one of your own blood to be butchered by the redskin?

SCUDDER. Hold on now, Jacob; we've got to figure on that—let us look straight at the thing. Here we are on the selvage[1] of civilization. It ain't our sile, I believe, rightly; but Nature has said that where the white man sets his foot, the red man and the black man shall up sticks and stand around. But what do we pay for that possession? In cash? No—in kind—that is, in protection, forbearance, gentleness, in all them goods that show the critters the difference between the Christian and the savage. Now, what have you done to show them the distinction? for, darn me if I can find out.

M'CLOSKY. For what I have done, let me be tried.

SCUDDER. You have been tried—honestly tried and convicted. Providence has chosen your executioner. I shan't interfere.

PETE. Oh, no; Mas'r Scudder, don't leave Mas'r Closky like dat—don't sa—'tain't what good Christian should do.

SCUDDER. D'ye hear that, Jacob? This old nigger, the grandfather of the boy you murdered, speaks for you—don't that go through you? D'ye feel it? Go on, Pete, you've waked up the Christian here, and the old hoss responds. (*Throws bowie knife to* M'CLOSKY.) Take that, and defend yourself.

(*Exit* SCUDDER *and* PETE—WAHNOTEE *faces* M'CLOSKY—*Fight.* M'CLOSKY *runs off*—WAHNOTEE *follows him*—*Screams outside.*)

---

1   *selvage* Fringe.

SCENE 4. *Parlor at Terrebonne. Enter* ZOE. *Music.*

ZOE. My home, my home! I must see you no more. Those little
flowers can live, but I cannot. Tomorrow they'll bloom the
same—all will be here as now, and I shall be cold. Oh! my
life, my happy life; why has it been so bright? (*Enter* MRS.
PEYTON *and* DORA.)

DORA. Zoe, where have you been?

MRS. P. We felt quite uneasy about you.

ZOE. I've been to the negro quarters. I suppose I shall go before
long, and I wished to visit all the places, once again, to see the
poor people.

MRS. P. Zoe, dear, I'm glad to see you more calm this morning.

DORA. But how pale she looks, and she trembles so.

ZOE. Do I? (*Enter* GEORGE.) Ah! he is here.

DORA. George, here she is.

ZOE. I have come to say goodbye, sir; two hard words—so hard
they might break many a heart, mightn't they?

GEORGE. Oh, Zoe! can you smile at this moment?

ZOE. You see how easily I have become reconciled to my fate—so
it will be with you. You will not forget poor Zoe! but her
image will pass away like a little cloud that obscured your
happiness a while—you will love each other; you are both too
good not to join your hearts. Brightness will return amongst
you. Dora, I once made you weep; those were the only tears I
caused anybody. Will you forgive me?

DORA. Forgive you—(*Kisses her.*)

ZOE. I feel you do, George.

GEORGE. Zoe, you are pale. Zoe!—she faints!

ZOE. No; a weakness, that's all—a little water. (DORA *gets water.*)
I have a restorative here—will you pour it in the glass? (DORA
attempts to take it.) No; not you—George. (GEORGE *pours
contents of phial in glass.*) Now, give it to me. George, dear
George, do you love me?

GEORGE. Do you doubt it, Zoe?

ZOE. No! (*Drinks.*)

DORA. Zoe, if all I possess would buy your freedom, I would
gladly give it.

ZOE. I am free! I had but one Master on earth, and he has given me my freedom!

DORA. Alas! but the deed that freed you was not lawful.

ZOE. Not lawful—no—but I am going to where there is no law—where there is only justice.

GEORGE. Zoe, you are suffering—your lips are white—your cheeks are flushed.

ZOE. I must be going—it is late. Farewell, Dora. (*Retiring.*)

PETE. (*Outside.*) Whar's Missus—whar's Mas'r George?

GEORGE. They come.

(*Enter* SCUDDER.)

SCUDDER. Stand around and let me pass—room thar! I feel so big with joy, creation ain't wide enough to hold me. Mrs. Peyton, George Peyton, Terrebonne is yours. It was that rascal M'Closky—but he got rats, I swow[1]—he killed the boy, Paul, to rob this letter from the mailbags—the letter from Liverpool you know—he set fire to the shed—that was how the steamboat got burned up.

MRS. P. What d'ye mean?

SCUDDER. Read—read that. (*Gives letter.*)

GEORGE. Explain yourself.

(*Enter* SUNNYSIDE.)

SUNNYSIDE. Is it true?

SCUDDER. Every word of it, Squire. Here, you tell it, since you know it. If I was to try I'd bust.

MRS. P. Read, George. Terrebonne is yours.

(*Enter* PETE, DIDO, SOLON, MINNIE *and* GRACE.)

PETE. Whar is she—whar is Miss Zoe?

SCUDDER. What's the matter?

PETE. Don't ax me. Whar's de gal? I say.

SCUDDER. Here she is—Zoe!—water—she faints.

PETE. No—no. 'Tain't no faint—she's a dying, sa; she got pizon from old Dido here, this mornin'.

---

1   *swow* Swear.

GEORGE. Zoe!

SCUDDER. Zoe! is this true?—no, it ain't—darn it, say it ain't. Look here, you're free, you know; nary a master to hurt you now; you will stop here as long as you've a mind to, only don't look so.

DORA. Her eyes have changed color.

PETE. Dat's what her soul's gwine to do. It's going up dar, whar dere's no line atween folks.

GEORGE. She revives.

ZOE. (*On sofa.*) George—where—where—

GEORGE. Oh, Zoe! what have you done?

ZOE. Last night I overheard you weeping in your room, and you said, "I'd rather see her dead than so!"

GEORGE. Have I then prompted you to this?

ZOE. No; but I loved you so, I could not bear my fate; and then I stood between your heart and hers. When I am dead she will not be jealous of your love for me, no laws will stand between us. Lift me; so—(GEORGE *raises her head.*)—let me look at you, that your face may be the last I see of this world. Oh! George, you may, without a blush, confess your love for the Octoroon. (*Dies.* GEORGE *lowers her head gently. Kneels. Others form picture.*)

(*Darken front of house and stage. Light fires.—Draw flats and discover* PAUL'S *grave.—*M'CLOSKY *dead on it.—*WAHNOTEE *standing triumphantly over him.*)

—1859

In Context

American Reviews

"'The Octoroon.' A Disgrace to the North, a Libel[1] on the South,"
Spirit of the Times; A Chronicle of the Turf, Agriculture, Field Sports,
Literature and the Stage (**17 December 1859**)

> This review is reproduced in full because it provides a range of infor-
> mation about attitudes to race, class, and other social problems, as
> well as details about the original performance itself. This is perhaps
> the most vitriolic review of the play, representing the types of objec-
> tions shared by the play's American critics. The language and attitudes
> towards race and class may be extremely offensive to modern readers,
> but are a historical reality that cannot be ignored or forgotten.

It is a significant fact, that while at one end of the La Farge House
a few gentlemen were discussing the propriety of getting up a meet-
ing in this city to prove that the North was entirely abolitionized,
the other end of the same building was occupied by the rehearsal of
a five-act play, the effect of which is to misrepresent and villify the
South; and it is also a significant fact, that while the object discussed
by the "conservative," has been treated by the public with singular
indifference, a gross libel upon the social relations of the South has
been hailed, by a part of the press, and a gaping multitude, with an
"unparalled enthusiasm."

"The Winter Garden"—a very appropriate term for this dreary
theatre, for there has never been a really green spot in its history—has
been struggling, under the management of Dion Bourcicault,[2] all the
season to sustain itself by the representation of Cockney plays. The
legitimate attractions of the house, it seems, finally proved abortive,

---

1 *Libel* Legal term used to describe a false published statement that is damaging to a reputa-
   tion.
2 *Bourcicault* All references to Boucicault's name in the US use the alternative spelling of
   "Bourcicault," a spelling used by the author himself, as seen in letters to newspaper editors.

and as a last resource, Bourcicault has taken advantage of the existing anti-Southern excitement, for it is no longer aimed at the slave, but at the citizens of the South, to bring out a play which, for all practical purposes, is more pernicious than anything which has heretofore been conceived in the spirit of sectional hate. "Uncle Tom's Cabin"[1] aspired to no higher aim than to represent that plausible thing, *a heavenly old negro*! and an impossibly bad white man. The hero of the play, however, was "a darkie," the legitimate representative of the American slave; but Bourcicault is not content with this, his Exeter Hall[2] training has carried him further; he has been made familiar with white slaves in his own country, so he dares to represent them in this. As false as the incidents of the play are in fact and in sentiment, as a literary composition it is wretchedly bad, judged even by the low standard applied to all the modern trash of the Bourcicault school, the materials that were worth attending to being miserably managed, the plot and the dramatic effect implying a total want of ingenuity; all the author has evidently relied upon being the *excitement* and *inflammatory* effect that its representations would produce, rather than any really theatrical merit. The scene, says the elaborate play-bill advertised in the daily papers, "is laid in the Delta of the Mississippi, on the plantation of Terrebonne;" the name of the planter is "Peyton," the place itself is "Sunnyside." All Louisiana names certainly, which would naturally be made familiar with Bourcicault, while acting as a New Orleans theatrical manager, the recipient of Southern hospitality and a witness of Southern city life, but with the names all correctness and truthful localization ceases. The natural representations are always false, and the characters are, with one exception, libelous. In the first scene, an alluvial plantation,[3] which is as free from pebbles as a cup-custard, is faced in the foreground with huge piles of rock that would be formidable even in New England, while a tall palm waves over them, which is as unknown in Louisiana as in Labrador.

To give our readers a slight idea of the gross exaggeration, we will notice that the play opens with Jacob McCloskey, "half-owner of the Terrebonne estate," say worth a hundred thousand dollars; with Sa-

---

1 *Uncle Tom's Cabin* Popular 1852 anti-slavery novel written by Harriet Beecher Stowe.
2 *Exeter Hall* Building in London where meetings of the Anti-Slavery Society were often held.
3 *alluvial plantation* Plantation in a river valley with rich, fertile soil.

lem Scudder, the overseer of the Terrebonne estate; and George Peyton, a Southern young man, "educated in Europe, and just returned home," all in love with Zoe, the octoroon, and all severally making love to her, and *offering their hand in marriage*! In rude language, in the first act, three white men, two of independent fortune, and one with character enough to be an overseer on a large estate, seriously propose to "marry a nigger." This is Bourcicault's idea of Southern institutions, and this idea is the English and the Wendell Phillips[1] idea, to endeavor, by false sympathy, to break down caste, and elevate the negro to the same level with the whites.

To accomplish this object, Miss Agnes Robertson,[2] who is a pretty Scotch woman of a singularly pure complexion, dressed in snowy muslin, and overflowing with sentiment and sensitiveness, is the octoroon. To render the thing even more offensive, her parentage is freely discussed by the ladies of the household, her free papers talked about, while, meantime, instead of acting the part of the servant, this Bourcicault heroine is receiving, as we have already intimated, serious proposals of marriage, from the gentlemen, and being enveloped in the arms of Mrs. Judge Peyton, who is familiar with her origin and her mixed blood. Dora Sunnyside is held up as a Southern belle, and here Mrs. Allen, a very handsome delicate beauty, comes on the stage, slatternly dressed, and so inanimate, so overcome by lassitude, that she can scarcely keep from "dissolving away." This caricature upon Southern young ladies thus moves along, only to be awakened from her lethargy to *make love* to George Peyton, who had previously sworn to sacrifice fortune and all for the love of the octoroon! and who frankly tells the "Southern belle" that his heart is already engaged by what seems to us to be the "yaller gal." If offensive caricature of the South, and of the most sacred ties of life can go further than this, we do not recollect the example. Among the male characters we have prominently "Jules Thibodeaux, a young Creole planter," bearing one of the most honored names among the old French population, answering to our Livingtons and Lees, of the North; this "young planter" is personated by Miss H. Secor, who has the manners of a "Dead Rabbit," and in the meanwhile is persistently smoking an execrable segar,[3] the

---

1   *Wendell Phillips*   American abolitionist, politician, and lawyer (1811-84).
2   *Agnes Robertson*   Boucicault's wife.
3   *segar*   Cigar.

offensive odor of which sickens the audience located in the remotest parts of the house.

Wah-no-tee is an Indian "of the Lepan tribe," an aborigine, as far as dress is concerned, such as you see in lady book illustrations. Now the Lepans were a terrible flat-headed tribe originated in Grub-street, London; the natives natural to the vicinity of Terrebonne, La, have been exterminated at least one hundred and fifty years, and were known as the Houmas and the Attakapas. Wah-no-tee, however, is a wonderful creation, written expressly to display the acting dramatic power of Bourcicault, who has nothing to do but drink whiskey and flourish a large club; not understanding English, he despairs of conversation, and naturally confines himself to guttural sounds, a large "whew!" such as a bear makes when suddenly come upon by a pack of dogs, is all he has to say, but his head-dress and tail-feathers are immense.

Salem Scudder is a Yankee from Massachusetts, and holds the position of an overseer, whose slang about "civilization" and "human rights," joined with his nasal twang, would cause him to be run out of any decent community in Louisiana as a disagreeable associate for Southern gentlemen, and an exemplar of bad manners before negroes.

Now the above is a fair representation of the prominent persons in the play, announced as representing "American characters, American scenes, and *Southern* homes!" the minor parts being filled up with vulgarisms of all sorts, miserable white men, women, and children, blackened up to represent field hands and house servants.

The dialogue opens with McClosky, a fine example of a Baltimore "Blood Tub,"[1] announcing his intention to "degrade the pride of the first families," a sentient thoroughly sympathized in by the Yankee, who has his fling at the "chivalry." McClosky, in the course of the piece, meets with Zoe, announces the ruin of the Southern family, makes love to her, and "being despised by that interesting creature, very naturally decides "he will buy her at the sale." By a series of ridiculous and puerile "actions and plots," he manages to bring the estate to the hammer, thereby introducing the "negro sale," which our city papers, even those that try to be very fair to the South, with

---

1 *Baltimore "Blood Tub"* In Baltimore, Maryland, in the 1850s, Blood Tubs were gangs whose methods of attacking their political opponents included submerging them in tubs of blood collected from slaughterhouses.

one or two honorable exceptions, pronounce "wonderfully life-like." Here is a chance for broad misrepresentation. White women, men, and children, are artfully dressed to produce effective groups—husbands are sold, and there spring up discussions among the buyers about separating them from their wives and children; the auctioneer "diversifying the bids" with asking for tobacco and "brandy smashes;" quarrels ensue, and bowies and pistols are most awkwardly drawn, the Yankee flourishing a big jack-knife and awkwardly "cavorting about," until it seemed to us strange that the beings who were enacting this outrage upon a section of the Union, had not thrown this fellow out the window in sheer and seriously felt disgust. Finally comes the climax; Miss Agnes Robertson, for it was her the audience saw, was put on the block for sale. That such an exhibition was offensive, there cannot be a doubt, but that it should be for a moment taken as a representation of Southern life as disgusting, and those who desire it should be so understood are guilty of the worst kind of treason.

The degraded and ignorant beings who are trafficked in by the South have none of the sentiments and feelings accorded to Zoe; in that country, if such a being as Zoe ever existed in person, her mind and the taint of her blood would create a gulf between her and the whites that would be wider than the poles asunder; and all the sympathy and sentiment the incendiary author of this piece creates, is founded upon the false idea that there is an equality in the races, an idea that is preposterous, unnatural, and profane.

Starting from the theatre after the sale of Miss Robertson, and reflecting upon the fact, how miserably cheap the crowded audience was also "sold," as exhibited by their expressions of sympathy, we ran against a multitude of the poor victims of Northern society, who were driven by the lash of necessity along the gas-lighted streets and standing *for sale* at every corner.

These victims of oppression, of bad laws, and of the "inhumanity of man to man," were pure-blooded whites, and in their veins coursed the purest fountains of blood. Their fathers and mothers are free, and in many instances, people of consideration, and estate. These wretched Zoes of the North, have no negro taint; they are often full of womanly tenderness, of refined natures, have been in many instances nursed as the pet of the Christian family circle, have read and appreciated Milton and Shakespeare, have hung with rapture over the preductions of the inspired pencil—are in fact *white women* doomed to inevitable servitude and degradation, compared with which the sufferings of the Southern Zoe, even of the worst possible estate, would be heavenly in comparison. Yet these Northern slaves, to say nothing of the thousands of children of infirm women, of aged men, who fill our almshouses,[1] and crowded walks, have not a tear dropped for their condition, every one of whom would be happy, could they enjoy the daily comforts which are at the command of the least favored of the Southern slaves. Nay, worse than this, white women, without protest or sympathy, are not only heartlessly and openly sold in the streets of our Northern towns, but whole families of high respectability are bid off at prices which would hardly pay in Charleston or New Orleans for a likely-looking coachman, three thousand dollars being deemed by a Boston jury quite enough for a seducer to pay for the crushed hopes and honest affections of a kind husband, the disgrace of innocent children, and a mother's blasted fame, the whole family circle, according to Bourcicault's play, going for thirty-seven thousand dollars less than the single physically and mentally degraded Octoroon brought at a Southern auction mart.

We have no disposition to pursue this disgusting subject further; the fact is patent that the play is nightly greeted by a crowded audience, and the basest attack that has yet been made upon the South is likely not only to do its damaging work in poisoning the minds of our people, but will possess the additional sin of putting money in the pockets of the base creatures who have clubbed together their mercenary brains to put together this outrage.

For this the press is much to blame; the criticisms which have been written on this play, even in the best quarters, have been characterized by a secret desire to sustain it, or have been the result of willful and besotted ignorance. As an abstract dramatic presentation, it would not live a second night, but when the papers applaud, or in feebly denouncing, always add, it is a true picture of the South, they give it the only endorsement that carries weight and makes it "draw." So entirely reprehensible, and so consistent is this hypocritical course, that the "*Times*" of Tuesday last, although it had several announcements denouncing the fanatics of the North, and deploring sectional

---

1   *almshouses*   Charitable housing institutions.

agitation, and seemingly ambitious to be very fair and conservative, yet in its notice, in another column, of the "Octoroon," it is careful to say, that the play is a "MODERATE *and truthful picture of Southern life*," thus, in a line, showing its real sentiments of the South and Southern people.

We pronounce again the whole play a libel; it is more false than if a Southern theatrical manager should bring out at New Orleans or Charleston, a play in which the degraded men and women, and an association of the vilest stews of New York city were produced, and called a "moderate and truthful picture of the best Northern life." This representation would be true, at least, of much Northern life, but the "Octoroon" has not a glimpse, if we except old Uncle "Pete," that can with truth be termed characteristic of Southern life and Southern homes.

from "The Octoroon" *The Charleston Courier, Tri-Weekly* (22 December 1859)

The bulk of this article is a summary of the *Spirit of the Times* review, and its emphatic language indicates the reporter's outrage towards Boucicault's play. The fact that it is not a review, but a news report, indicates the seriousness of the perceived offense committed against the South by Boucicault. The following is a brief excerpt.

... The object of the author of this play is to throw ridicule and contempt upon the prejudice existing in the South against color. It has had a successful run, delighted vast numbers of men and women, for which refining pleasure they have cheerfully filled the greedy pockets of base caterers to their low tastes. It is composed of stupid caricatures and gross misrepresentations of Southern life, manners and sentiment, and notwithstanding it abounds in all manner of barefaced lies, and is beneath contempt as an artistic and literary composition. ...This is the sort of food on which the Northern public, the controlling spirits of that section, are fed. It is on pictures such as this they are told to gaze and inflame their hatred of their *dear* brethren of the South. And yet the press is silent, and the vile lie is taken for truth.

from "Winter Garden—First Night of 'The Octoroon,'" *The New York Herald* (7 December 1859)

> This review is far more favorable than the first two, but is ambivalent in its final judgment. The *Herald* was a pro-slavery paper.

The first strictly original work that has been produced at this theatre under the present management, was presented last night to a crowded house.

It is a serio-comic drama, in five acts, written by Mr. Bourcicault, the most prolific and the most successful among the English dramatists of the day. The title of the new piece is "The Octoroon, or Life in Louisiana." The dramatist deals with the events and the characters of today, and his play touches directly upon the most delicate phases of the most important social and political question now agitated by the people of this country. In view of the exceeding interest which this play has excited, we give a detailed analysis of its plot, as follows:[1] ...

This, it will be seen, is a strong and effective plot. The dialogue is very terse. Not an unnecessary word is used from the beginning to the end. The characters are clearly and sharply defined, and the author has caught in such types as Miss Sunnyside, Pete, Scudder and Pointdexter the exact *resemblance* to American life.

The octaroon [sic] and the rascally overseer are imaginative characters. Persons like them may or may not have existed. For the rest, for the arrangement of its details the play is exceedingly life-like, almost photographic in its exactness. In its presentation the greatest care had evidently been exercised. Down to the smallest detail of furniture, the *ensemble* was perfect. The characters were dressed and acted to the life. The best theatre in Paris could not have done better with an important work. Its reception by the audience was favorable, without being especially enthusiastic. The applause was a tribute to the clever acting and the fine *mise en scéne*, rather than an endorsement of the sentiments which the motive of the drama inculcates.

As it is our purpose to give today merely an outline of the play, we can devote but a few words to the artists who sustained the principal

---

1   *we give a detailed ... as follows*   An extended summary of the play's setting, plot, and dialogue occupies the bulk of this review.

Charles the Younger Coote, *Zoe the Octoroon Galop*, 1862.
This cover illustration shows Wahnotee as the central figure,
discovering Paul's bloody body with the river in the background.

rôles. We may say, however, in a general way, that every part was well and carefully played. The honors of the night will be given to Miss Agnes Robertson, who acted a part rather out of her line, gracefully, touchingly, and well; to Mrs. Allen, who completely filled her *rôle* looking and acting exceedingly well; to Mr. Jefferson, whose performance of Scudder was capital; to Mr. Jamieson (who was received with applause and cheers), and who played the old house servant exceedingly well; to Mrs. Allen, whose Dora was perfectly life-like in every way; and to Mr. Bourcicault, who "made up" as the technical phrase goes, admirably, and gave to the character of the Indian a due degree of aboriginal stolidity.

The audience received the play favorably, but not enthusiastically. The scenes we have quoted above and the fourth act were applauded. The fifth act is very simple, and was not liked. Whether or not "The Octoroon" will keep the stage is a matter for the public to decide.

English Reviews

"Saving the Octoroon," *Punch* (21 December 1861)

As always, *Punch* had a comic response to current topics—here, the passionate discussion among theater-goers about the unacceptability of *The Octoroon*'s tragic ending. In suggesting that the suicide could be easily prevented if Zoe was given the news about the recovered letter, the poem also points to some of the key criticisms of melodrama: false dilemmas and the forced timing that leads to tragic or happy consequences.

Saving the Octoroon

Upon the couch she lies so pale—
   'Tis but a graceful swoon;
What? Poison?—nay—'tis sure a tale,
He'll never thus our hearts assail,
   And kill the *Octoroon*!

Say, BOUCICAULT, that she survives!
   Grant us this public boon;
If cats are blessed with nine-fold lives,
Give two to her, this pearl of wives,
   Don't kill the *Octoroon*!

There still is time; that negress might
   By the uncertain moon,
A phial give, which though to sight
The same, would op'rate different quite,
   Nor kill the *Octoroon*?

McClosky fall'n by Indian blow,
   (Or to fall very soon)
Cannot appear to bid her go,
Then why that fact not let her know,
   And save the *Octoroon*.

True *Peyton* has another flame,
    Is somewhat of a spoon;
But give him up, Miss What's-your-name,
You must admit 't'would be a shame,
    To kill the *Octoroon*.

So say I, and the public voice
    Sings to the self-same tune,
It's not as if you had no choice—
Why break the hearts you can rejoice?
    Why kill the *Octoroon*?

Don't tell us that the thing must be,
    You're far too cute a 'coon;
To be so reg'lar up a tree,
You can't find a catastrophe
    That saves the *Octoroon*.

Of law supreme, fate, and such rot,
    Preach on from this to June;
I say—necessity or not—
Poor Zoe must not go to pot—
    Don't kill the *Octoroon*.

What if your logic comes to grief,
    When thus your play you prune?
I still insist on the relief,
Both to my nerves and handkerchief—
    Don't kill the *Octoroon*.

Untruth to manners I'll admit,
    Though clear as sun at noon;
"Anything else we'll stand or sit,
But this," cry boxes, gallery and pit,
    "Don't kill the *Octoroon*."

The author heard; he rubbed his chin;
    "They'll call me a poltroon.[1]
But if her death the houses thin,
Perhaps 'tis time I should begin
    To save the *Octoroon.*"

"Tragic necessity, good-bye—
    And manners change your tune
The public voice I'll ratify—
My pretty *Zoe* shall not die—
    I'll save the *Octoroon.*

'Tis said; 'tis done; and now the play
    Goes blithe as songs of June:
Miss What's-her-name's put out o'way,
Zoe weds *George.* Hip! Hip! Hooray!
    We've saved the *Octoroon!*

from "Theatres and Music," *John Bull* (Saturday, 23 November 1861)

The following two reviews represent the typical English reviewer's response to the betrayal of the English audiences' expectations of a happy ending after enduring the many crises to which the melodramatic
hero and heroine are subjected. *John Bull*'s reviewer also takes care
to distance England from slave-owning culture, declaring the South's
principles of ethnic separation so alien to English audiences that they
find it impossible to grasp the logic and seriousness of Zoe's dilemma.

The long promised drama of *The Octoroon* was produced at the Adelphi Theatre on Monday night, before an audience who filled the
house in every part, and who were evidently prepared for another
"sensation" such as was created by the *Colleen Bawn.*[2] The appearance
of a new piece by the author of that drama almost necessitates con-
siderations on the subject of its extraordinary success. Certainly, even

---

1   *poltroon*   Coward.
2   *Colleen Bawn*   Melodramatic play by Dion Boucicault first performed 27 March 1860 in
    New York.

by the keenest and most appreciative of our critics the unprecedented success of the *Colleen Bawn* was not anticipated....

No doubt a great part of the audience on Monday night expected an impossibility. They required that the new piece on its first night should have all the cumulative effect of the previous success, and anything short of that would have disappointed them, as *Octoroon* probably did. In one respect the author was fortunate; he had fresh ground to break, and the story and the incidents of the new piece are such as almost preclude comparisons; in another he was unfortunate, as he seems to have felt when he explained in the advertisements the meaning of his title, and the law which his plot turned upon. The danger of a drowning heroine[1] needs no such explanation; and here is the weak point in the new piece—a weakness which no skill of construction or power of dramatic writing could overcome. The British public are practically so unacquainted with a state of society in which a white man is prevented by law of marrying a woman who may have a drop of black blood in her veins, that they cannot be brought to interest themselves in a hero and heroine whose difficulties arise from the existence of such a legal impediment, nor can they see with any great amount of sympathy the force of such a sacrifice as a heroine committing suicide in order to put an end to the difficulty. The basis of the story of the new drama is indicated by the above remarks, and the plot is carried on by a series of incidents in themselves most ingeniously invented and arranged, and by means of which up to the end of the fourth act the interest of the audience is kept alive. The principal characters are the Octoroon herself, the daughter of a deceased planter, who has neglected some legal formalities necessary to her complete manumission;[2] her lover, the planter's nephew; two stewards, who have contributed to ruin the planter's estate—the one a villain, the other a Yankee schemer, but honest—both in love with the Octoroon; an old negro, drawn with great skill; an Indian who hangs about the estate; a Quadroon boy; and a dashing young lady—a Southern belle, herself most anxious to marry the planter's nephew. The chief incidents are the murder of the Quadroon boy to secure possession of a letter by the villainous steward, who is accidentally photographed in the act; a sale of the

---

1   *heroine*   Eily O'Connor, the *Colleen Bawn*.
2   *manumission*   Slave owner's act of formally freeing a slave.

slaves on the planter's estate, a scene new to our stage, and worked up with great dramatic skill; and a scene outside a river steamer, where the Indian is accused of murdering the Quadroon boy, and is about to be lynched, only that the Yankee undertakes his defence, and the photograph being discovered at the crisis of his fate, the tables are turned upon the steward, who, however, contrives to escape by setting fire to the steamer, the burning of which closes the fourth act. In the fifth, which is unnecessarily prolonged by two scenes at least, there is the pursuit of the steward by the Indian, resulting in his death and the suicide of the Octoroon just as the family she belonged to are rescued from their difficulties. This tragical termination appeared to be very much to the distaste of the audience, and it weakened greatly the effect produced by earlier portions of the drama. For the acting, it was throughout excellent. Mrs. Boucicault evidenced great concentrated power as the Octoroon; and Mrs. Marston, as the planter's widow, was quiet and impressive. A lady from America, Mrs. Latimer, played the not easy part of the southern belle with discrimination and good feeling; and Miss Clara Denvil, a child, gave an interesting reality to the poor Quadroon boy. Mr. Boucicault is as good a Yankee as he is an Irishman—no mean praise, and Mr. Emery gave a forcible portrait of the scoundrelly steward, running almost to tragedy in the later scenes of exhaustion and horror at the implacable vengeance of the Indian, who was acted with a good deal of melodramatic power by Mr. Phillips, another importation from the American stage. But the character which was the greatest novelty in the cast, and which, as it proved, excited in the highest degree the approval of the audience, was that of the old "nigger," in which Mr. Jameson, his first appearance here, produced a remarkable effect. Such a negro portrait we have never had before, impossible to be characterized, and yet played with such variety of detail and such force as compel a ready acceptance of it as a completely true picture. The landscape portions of the scenery are not so well painted as they might be, although characteristic, and in a certain manner effective, and the audience without doubt disappointed in the destruction of the steamer, which was evidently looked forward to, but in vain, as a climax of effect. As a whole *The Octoroon* is one of the best dramas that had been produced for some years, the fullest of incident and character, and the best acted, and despite its faults ought to prove a great success. It was received with every mark of approbation.

from "Adelphi" (Review of *The Octoroon*), *The Athenaeum*
(23 November 1861)

After many postponements, the new sensation-drama was produced on Monday. *The Octoroon* is one of a series of plays which have been tried and proved by Mr. Boucicault, in America, as remarkably effective with that mixed class of audiences which requires in a drama an exciting story, with a scene or two calculated to cause a thrilling sensation in the majority. And it is a "sensation" properly so called;—not an emotion of the mind, not a tragic feeling in response to passion, not sympathy with suffering or heroism, but the impression made on the nervous system by an actual occurrence passing before the sense, calculated to awaken fear or expectation, or wonder, and to give a shock, not always pleasant, to the frame. Here, as it were, the whole audience meet on the same level, receiving an impression affecting the lower powers of the mind, compounded of sights and sounds that cause a certain degree of apprehension for the safety of an individual, for whom a strong dramatic interest has been created. Mr. Boucicault has reduced the means of producing such an effect to an art; and, by calling in the scene-painter and machinist to his aid, has augmented the effect in a manifold manner.

… This is the exciting sensation-scene;—the bidding for the poor girl, and the determined outbidding by the remorseless villain, whose lawless love is her ruin. This scene is most skillfully handled;—there is neither exaggeration nor apparent seeking for effect in it;—but it is a literal representation of such transactions in the South, and tells all the more forcibly by reason of its naked truth. Justice, as we have said, comes up at last with M'Closkey, who is confined in the hold of a steamer, but, while there, contrives to throw a lighted lantern among some tar-barrels,[1] and to escape in the confusion consequent on the conflagration. He falls, however, into the power of the Indian, who sacrifices him on the grave of little Paul. The packet, also, reaches the hands of Peyton, but too late;—for poor Zoe has, in her despair, taken poison.

It is probable that this tragic ending will somewhat impair the popularity of the new drama; for mixed audiences, after having enjoyed the sensations that accompany the presence of danger, expect a happy

---

1   *tar-barrels*   Large barrels soaked in tar.

deliverance, as a reward for the terrors they have voluntarily suffered, and, if denied this, are apt to regard themselves as defrauded of their due rights. Some such feeling was manifested at the conclusion of this exciting drama. But the elegance of the dialogue, the novelty of the situations, and the merit of the acting, particularly on the part of Mrs. Boucicault, had already extorted an abundance of applause, and the curtain fell upon an unquestionable triumph. For the rest, the beauty of the scenery, and the general completeness of the accessories, will secure it a prolonged success if the steamer on fire do not, some night, prove more "sensational" than was originally intended.

Playbill for the Adelphi (London, UK)
production of *The Octoroon*, 1861.

"Pan at the Play," *Fun* **(Saturday, 30 November 1861)**

Of course every playgoer knows by this time the plot of the *Octoroon*, and that the audience after applauding through four acts, became squeamish at the conclusion, and hailed the descent of the curtain with anything but a congratulatory accompaniment. The picture of a heroine dying by poison, administered to her in ignorance of its dreadful property, is not a pleasant one, and the opening of the scene at the back to exhibit a supernatural picture is an injudicious effect which is altogether out of place in a drama which, if it is to succeed, must do so from its naturalness and the vivid truth of its transatlantic pictures. It is a strange sight to watch an English audience on the first night of an important dramatic production, to see how thoroughly they ignore the effects of the earlier portion of the play, and how swayed they are by the concluding incidents and tableau.[1] Anybody who has witnessed the first four acts of the *Octoroon* on Monday, and was compelled to leave after so doing, would have felt perfectly certain as to its success. But, alas! what may not happen in a short half-hour; one unpleasant situation, or an unskillfully worked-up climax, will peril, or perhaps destroy, the hopes of the most brilliant dramatist and the most experienced and effective company. Notwithstanding the uncomfortable feeling induced by the final act, the *Octoroon* will draw, and will prove, if not a second *Colleen Bawn*, at all events a remunerative and sufficiently successful production.

"Adelphi Theatre" (Review of Revised Play), *The Times* **[London] (12 December 1861)**

> The following two reviews approvingly acknowledge Boucicault's decision to bow to the pressure from English reviewers and audiences and give *The Octoroon* a happy ending. The tone of the reviewers of *The Times* and *Fun*, and the satirical poet of *Punch* (see above) suggests the audiences' deep emotional investment in Zoe's fate.

The Octoroon dies no more! When she first died, a few weeks since, the audience did not like it, but her author, Mr. Boucicault, stoutly maintained the proprieties of Louisiana, though her death, night after

---

1   *tableau*   Formation of posed actors at the end of a scene.

night, was not only deplored, but disapproved. There was a strong case on both sides. Mr. Boucicault was aware that a marriage between a white man and a woman of colour would be regarded in a Slave State as something abominable, even in the absence of legal prohibition. The public, on the other hand, did not see why the gallant George Peyton should not bring the beautiful Zoe over to England, where neither the laws of the land nor of society would thwart his inclinations. Mr. Boucicault saw in the peculiar position of the coloured race across the Atlantic the basis for as sharp a tragic collision as might be exhibited in some legend of classical antiquity. The public, on the contrary, did not want a tragedy at all, but insisted that, when once the bad man of the story was killed, the curtain ought to descend on a picture of universal happiness.

Mr. Boucicault has at last, yielded, and, as we have said, the Octoroon dies no more. Nay, she does not even think of dying, and the fifth act of the melodrama has been so thoroughly reconstructed that those who see it for the first time in its new shape will be puzzled to conjecture how the unpopular incident was brought about. She is now carried off by the wicked M'Closky, and when she is rescued from his clutches by George Peyton and a body of pursuers, it is explained that she and her lover will seek refuge in some happy country where the "sacrament of love" may take place without impediment. M'Closky is, of course, killed, but it is at the end of a complicated rifle skirmish, in the course of which the intrepid Yankee Salem (again played by Mr. Boucicault) receives a shot in the leg. The wound, however, is not sufficiently serious to prevent him from marrying Miss Dora, and so consoling her for the loss of George. Thus the curtain drops merrily on a brace of prospective weddings, instead of gloomily veiling over a scene of death and desolation.

It is worthy of notice that the preservation of the Octoroon's life coincides with the commencement of the Cattle Show. Was it surmised that the provincial heart was even more sensitive than the metropolitan to the sufferings of a lady in distress, and that where a townsman was grimly dissatisfied a countryman would have been obstreperously indignant? Happily, the experiment has not been made, the piece terminates amid shouts of unequivocal applause, and there is not a man brought to London by the annual show in Baker-street who has witnessed the death of the beautiful Octoroon.

A man who acknowledges his errors and amends his plays deserves the success Mr. Boucicault has met with in altering the last act, or rather writing a new last act, to the sensation drama of the *Octoroon*. By saving the life of the charming Zoe, the dramatist has paid a graceful compliment to the critics who recommended him to do so, and has strengthened his otherwise very powerful and effective play. Now that piece ends happily, bygones should be allowed to be bygones, but I must be permitted to give—as the late Charles Mathews said in his tortoiseshell tomcat song—one "long, last, lingering look" at the picture of the self-sacrificing heroine, and to exclaim, "positively for the last time," what *were* you thinking Mr. Boucicault, when you determined on that never-to-be-sufficiently-condemned tableau?

Letters to Editors Concerning the Lawsuit

"The Octoroon Conflict: Financial and Political View of the Case— Letter from Mrs. Agnes Robertson Bourcicault,"[1] *The New York Herald* (Friday, 16 December 1859)

To the Editor of the *Herald*.

Sir—I have withdrawn from the Winter Garden; but my reasons for doing so have been incorrectly stated in your journal of this morning. Yesterday I wrote to the management as follows:—

To W. Stuart, Esq.:—Sir—I decline to appear any more in the "Octoroon." I regret to find that the piece has given offence to a portion of the public, and my part in it especially. I receive continuously letters threatening me with violence, and when I go on the stage I do so in fear of some outrage to my self or to my husband. Therefore, I beg to withdraw the play.

Yours, truly,

Agnes Robertson Bourcicault.

The press had pointed out the political tendency of the "Octoroon," and your journal especially had blamed its production of this unhappy crisis. Oppressed by the sense that many of the public regarded the play as you did; that I was the object of just censure, having received letters from many families in this city urging the withdrawal or alteration of the play; intimidated by letters threatening us with violence, as a woman, I could not hold the position which the management desired to compel me to endure. I felt that I was unconsciously made the instrument to wound the feelings of one part of the public to gratify the other. In every sense my position was a painful one. I will not permit my name (or my husband's, if I can help it), to be associated with any scheme to make money out of a political excitement— especially on such a subject as slavery and at such a moment as this.

---

1   *The Octoroon Conflict ... Robertson Bourcicault*   This is one of several series of exchanges made public by the parties involved in the lawsuit.

The "Octoroon" was not intended to succeed on such merits. In your notice this morning you state that it has produced me over thirteen hundred dollars for six performances. It is true; but I cannot consent to sell my own self-esteem and the good opinion of my friends at that or any price.

In reply to the above letter [to Stuart] the following was handed to my husband at four o'clock yesterday afternoon. It is written by Mr. Thomas C. Fields, the Public Administrator, to whom Mr. Stuart states he has assigned the Winter Garden—of which Mr. Fields claims to be the manager:—

Wednesday, 14 December 1859

My Dear Sir—Mr. Stuart has handed to me your note, the extents of which surprise me. You have entered into an engagement with me to give the services of your wife, yourself, and pieces on certain terms, which, by your acceptance of these terms, you have today under your hand ratified. I now [will present] the "Octoroon" this evening, and I shall await your answer [and] require Mrs. Bourcicault and yourself to perform in said piece, till six o'clock, when, if no satisfactory answer be received, I shall proceed to make such arrangements as may become necessary by reason of your refusal.
Yours, &c.,
Thomas C. Fields,
Trustee of the Winter Garden

On consultation, it was thought it might be better that I should perform last night, rather than cause any public inconvenience. Accordingly, at a few minutes before six o'clock I went to the Winter Garden, and was refused admission by the stage porter, who informed me that he had received orders from Mr. Fields not to admit me. I am, sir, your obliged servant,
Agnes Robertson Bourcicault
16 December 1859

A Selection of Letters from Boucicault Defending the Content of *The Octoroon*

"Letter from the Author of the 'Octoroon,'" *The New York Herald* (7 December 1859)

To the Editor of the *Herald*

I ask your permission to reply to one part of your editorial this morning upon my new work, "The Octoroon." After a residence of nearly seven years in this country—the seven happiest years of my life—I felt capable of writing a work upon society in America. I have laid the scene in the South, and, as slavery is an essential element of society there, insomuch I have been obliged to admit it into my scheme. But you say that it is a subject which should not be discussed by me at all in any form—that it should be interdicted to light literature and the drama. I profess to you sir, that I have so high an esteem for your judgment and the honesty of your convictions I cannot believe that you have considered this question with your usual fairness; and I think your desire to maintain peace and good will amidst the animosities which now unhappily disturb the republic has induced you to take a stand which your deliberate reflection will prompt you to relinquish. To keep the peace, you propose to knock down a bystander; to keep the peace, you would not only institute a censorship of the press—newspapers excepted—but you go further—you demand the subject shall not be mentioned; whether it be essential or not, it shall be avoided. I trust I have delicacy and good taste enough to refrain from treating any subject offensively, especially to a people who have treated me and mine with such kindness that to wound even their prejudices would be ingratitude; but I know, also, that I am man enough to speak out my heart; and if God has given me the talent to do so in a good work, I feel certain I shall not be denied that liberty which the meanest citizen of the United States claims as his birthright. I learned those rights chiefly from your columns, of which I have been a constant reader and admirer, nor the less so because you have occasionally scored me with the nib of your pen; but not until today have you taught me that a muzzle was the emblem of American freedom and the handcuffs symbols of its liberty. In pursuance of such a principle I may expect that some other morning journal will propose tomorrow that no person shall wear crape[1] on his white hat, as that circumstance may *provoke* a black idea. I believe the drama to be a proper and very effective instrument to use in the dissection of all social matters. The Greeks thought so, who founded it: Molière thought so when he wrote the "Tartuffe;"[2] and a very humble follower of theirs thinks so, too. It is by such means that the drama can be elevated into the social importance it deserves to enjoy. Therefore I have involved in "The Octoroon" sketches of slave life, truthful, I know, and I hope gentle and kind. My next subject for illustration will be the "Press," a comedy of character and intrigue, towards which I take advantage of this opportunity to solicit your flattering attention.

Dion Bourcicault
New York, 5 December 1859

"The Octoroon Gone Home," *New York Times*[3] (9 February 1860)

Gentlemen:

My work, "The Octoroon; or, Life in Louisiana," has been attacked by the Press here—some alleging that it is a rank pro-slavery drama, others that it is an Abolition play in disguise, and others that it is neither.

As for my political persuasion, I am a Democrat, and a Southern Democrat, but do not mix myself up with politics in any way; still when I found myself under an imputation of writing anything with

---

1   *crape*   Thin, crimped silk material used to adorn hats. Black crape is often worn as a symbol of mourning.
2   *Molière*   Jean-Baptiste Poquelin (1622-73), known more commonly by his stage name, Molière, was a French playwright and actor;   *Tartuffe*   Molière's 1664 comedy about religious hypocrisy was censored by King Louis XIV for its challenge to social institutions.
3   *New York Times*   These letters were reprinted in the *New York Times* after originally appearing in the New Orleans *Picayune*.

the smallest tendency against my convictions, I withdrew the work not because I disowned it—I withdrew it to send it down South that you might see for yourselves whether even inadvertently I could prostitute my abilities, my convictions and my feelings.

It is not probable that I shall ever visit the South again, so I am doubly anxious to retain the good opinion of the friends I made and left there. And I have no more honest, straight, and manly course to pursue than to send on the work as I do now, and prove by its representation that I am not unworthy to retain your kind remembrance.

I am, yours truly,
Dion Bourcicault
New York, 17 January 1860

To His Excellency the Governor of the State of Louisiana,

Sir: I have the honor to place before you a work of fiction, called "The Octoroon; or, Life in Louisiana." It has been represented in this City, and the reception it has met with from many Southern families of distinction, has induced me to dedicate to your Excellency a picture of plantation life, not the less faithful because drawn by one who feels so warmly towards the sunny South.

If its merits be humble, I trust its honesty and truth will recommend it to your favor. And let the absence of flattery from its pages attest the sincerity of my conviction.

Your Excellency's obedient servant,
Dion Bourcicault
New York, 17 January 1860

"'The Octoroon': To the Editor of the Times," *The Times* [London] (Wednesday, 20 November 1861)[1]

Sir,—In your criticism on my drama, *The Octoroon*, it is stated that the reception of the fifth act, in which the slave girl commits suicide in order to escape the embraces of the purchaser, contrasts strongly with the enthusiastic applause which had accompanied the first four acts of the play.

The question involved in these few words is not one of merely the craft of the playwright. I candidly admit that your estimate of public sympathy, as I expressed last night, is just as it is inexplicable. Since the Uncle Tom mania, the sentiments of the English public on the subject of slavery have seemed to be undergoing a great change; but I confess that I was not prepared to find that change so radical as it appeared to be when the experiment was tried upon the feelings of a miscellaneous audience. May I claim your attention to this view of a subject fraught with much serious intent?

A long residence in the Southern States of America had convinced me that the delineations in *Uncle Tom's Cabin* of the condition of the slaves, their lives, and feelings were not faithful. I found the slaves, as a race, a happy, gentle, kindly-treated population, and the restraints upon their liberty so slight as to be rarely perceptible. A visitor to Louisiana, who might expect to find his vulgar sympathies aroused by the exhibition of corporal punishment[2] and physical torture, would be much disappointed. For my part, with every facility for observation, I never witnessed any ill-treatment whatever of the servile class; on the contrary, the slaves are in general warmly attached to their masters and to their homes, and this condition of things I have faithfully depicted.

But behind all this there are features in slavery far more objectionable than any of those hitherto held up to human execration, by the side of which physical suffering appears as a vulgar detail. Some of these features are, for the first time, boldly exhibited in *The Octoroon*. The audience hailed this with every mark of enthusiasm the sunny views of negro life; they were pleased with the happy relations existing

---

1   *The Octoroon: To the Editor ... November 1861*   This important letter is cited frequently in scholarly studies.

2   *corporal punishment*   Physical punishment for a misdemeanor.

[b]etween the slaves and the family of which they were dependents; they enjoyed the heartiness with which these slaves were sold, and cheered the planters who bought them. But, when the Octoroon girl was purchased by the ruffianly[1] overseer to become his paramour,[2] her suicide to preserve her purity provoked no sympathy whatever. Yet, a few years ago, the same public, in the same theatre, witnessed with deep emotion the death of Uncle Tom under the lash, and accepted the tableau of the poor old negro, his shirt stained with the blood from his lacerated back, crawling across the stage, and dying in slow torture.

In the death of the Octoroon lies the moral and teaching of the whole work. Had this girl been saved, and the drama brought to a happy end, the horrors of her position, irremediable from the very nature of the institution of slavery, would subside into the condition of a temporary annoyance.

While I admit most fully the truth of your statement that the public was disappointed with the termination of the play, and would have been pleased with a happier issue, I feel strangely bewildered at such a change of feeling. Has public sentiment in this country veered so diametrically on this subject, and is it possible that this straw indicates the feeling of the English people is taking another course?

Yours respectfully,

Dion Boucicault
Hereford-house, 19 November 1861

---

1   *ruffianly*   Tough, rowdy, or violent.
2   *paramour*   Lover.

Boucicault on Acting

from Dion Boucicault, "The Art of Acting" (1882)

The importance to Boucicault of acting as a professional skill, and Boucicault's practical expertise in the profession, is evident from the body of lectures and speeches given by him on the subject, as well as from his role as an acting instructor in the last year of his life at New York's Madison Square Theater. A few years later, Boucicault's ideas about acting became part of a series of published discussions on dramatic craft. The French actor, Constant Coquelin's paper on acting, called "Actors and Acting" and published in May, 1887 in *Harper's Monthly*, started an exchange of letters and papers on acting by both Henry Irving (the first British actor to be knighted) and Dion Boucicault, each of whom clearly considered himself an expert in the field. In June 1887, Irving wrote a response to Coquelin's methods of acting in the journal, *Nineteenth Century*. In August 1887 Boucicault's article "Coquelin—Irving" appeared in the *North American Review*, and in November 1887, Coquelin replied to both Irving and Boucicault. Boucicault's perspective on the actor's art appears to have been in high demand for some time. The following excerpts, published in a collection called *Papers on Acting* (1922), are from a speech by Boucicault given at the Lyceum Theatre, and originally published in the *Era*, 29 July 1882.[1]

Now with regard to the voice, the secret of being heard is not a loud voice. I am not now speaking with a loud voice, yet I hope I am heard all over this place. "Yes." Thank you. Now I will tell you why. Because I have practised speaking articulately. Every syllable of every word is pronounced, and as far as I can every consonant and every vowel is pronounced. That is the secret of speaking plainly, speaking easily, and being heard in a large assembly. Now it is the vowel which gives support, and value, and volume to the consonants. When you want to give strong expression it is the consonant you go at, and not

---

1   *Era, 29 July 1882*   A weekly theatrical newspaper, *The Era* ran for approximately 100 years from 1838 to 1939.

the vowel; but when you want to be expressive, when you want to be agreeable, you go at your vowel.

The next thing a young actor has got to do is measure his breath. … All young actors fall off in the end of their phrases, and all go down in consequence. … The next thing for a young actor to study will be the letters l, m, n, and r, the four liquids in the alphabet—the four letters out of which you cannot possibly compose an unmusical word. … What have you English people done? One thing you have done is that you have abolished the letter r. Some people pronounce it like w. That is a misfortune they cannot help. But the majority of you, who are now laughing at those who pronounce it like w do not pronounce it at all. Some of you produce it as if it were an h, and when you are speaking of the Egyptian war, you say "the Egyptian wah!" and you say "that is rathah!" when you mean "rather" …

Then another fault of young actors and actresses is that they condense their words. Words having three syllables they put into two … they do not say "A Limited Liability Company: but "A Limted Libility Compny." … An old stager holds great stress on all the letters in order that he shall maintain the standard of purity and the proper pronunciation of the English language. There is another fault that young actors and actresses have, and that is they pronounce the letter i sometimes like oi, and sometimes a-eh. They talk of "Moi oie" or "Ma-eh a-eh" … In the better theatres and theatres of the first class, actors are kept in check in this respect, because acting managers are educated men, and therefore prevent actors from doing so; …

I will now … go to the question of the gesture. Now gesture on the stage must be distinct and deliberate. … the rule is that all gesture should precede slightly the words that it is to impress or to illustrate. … If I were to say "By heaven!" so [raising his arms after words],[1] that is comic, is it not?

… Another thing is, do not let your gesture be too short … [The spectator] does not like it, and does not understand that quick change.

… [T]he actor would reserve the last three or four words of his scene, and, walking to the [other] side [of the stage] would turn and speak those words to "take him off." So that twenty or thirty years ago

---

1   *[raising … after words]*   The insertions in square brackets appear to have been made by the editor of the *Era*.

an actor often said, "Would you give me a few words to take me off?" They could not get off the stage!

... The first lesson an actor has to learn is, not to speak. It is to learn to walk on the stage, stand still, and walk off again. ... his part is to listen, and if he can perform that part well—that is, the part of the listener—he will have achieved a progress in his art. ... Now, the finer part of the acting is to obtain an effect, not altogether what is given you to speak, but by listening to what another person speaks, and by its effect on you, by continuing your character while the other man is speaking.

... Many think they are studying their character when they are only studying themselves. ... Actors and actresses frequently come to me and say, "Have you any part that will fit me?" They never dream of saying, "Have you any part that I can fit? That I can expand and contract myself inside of; that I, as a Protean,[1] can shape myself into, even alter my voice and everything that nature has given to me, and be what you have contrived? I do not want you to continue like a tailor to fit me?" That is what is constantly happening.

... [T]he study of character should be done from the inside; not from the outside!

---

1 *Protean* Versatile and adaptable actor.

Alternative Endings

In the face of substantial criticism of the ending of *The Octoroon* from English audiences, several weeks into the play's run at London's Adelphi Theatre Boucicault revised the final act. The alternative ending—described by Boucicault as "composed by the Public, and edited by the Author"—does not appear to have survived. The following review from *The Illustrated London News* provides a summary of the melodramatic happy ending.

The Illustrated London News (14 December 1861)

The curtain rises, discovering the ruffian and his unfortunate slave in the cane-brake,[1] with the sun dawning over the Attakapas[2]—a beautiful scene. The ruffian is asleep, but he has secured his captive by tying her with a rope to a post, and when he awakes proceeds barbarously to compel her sharing with him all the dangers of his flight. Ultimately he is chased through the Red Cedar Swamp to the Painted Rocks, where he maintains his position from a rocky ledge against his assailants, having possessed himself of a gun with six charges, until he is brought down by a shot from George Peyton; Salem Scudder, by an act of self-sacrifice, having occasioned him to expose his body to Peyton's aim. The fair Octoroon is thus set at liberty, and the piece concludes with a declaration that in another land Zoe and Peyton will solemnise a lawful union, and live for the happiness of each other.

"Music and the Drama," *Bell's Life in London and Sporting Chronicle* (Sunday, 15 December 1861)

This summary provides more detail than that in *The Illustrated London News* review of 14 December 1861.

M'Closky endeavours to escape with the Octoroon, but is followed by George Peyton and his friends, by whom she is rescued, and to whom she is betrothed, and, as they cannot by reason of the law

---

1   *cane-brake*   Dense growth of sugar cane.
2   *Attakapas*   Former county in southern Louisiana.

marry in Louisiana, they depart for England, the land of the free, there to live happily. Salem also, though wounded in the skirmish, is consoled for the loss of Zoe by receiving Dora as his bride. The audience testified by their loud acclamations to their delight at this change in the *denouemens*,[1] and with this pleasant alteration we hope that Mr. Boucicault's drama may have a long and profitable run.

from *The Octoroon*: Founded on Dion Boucicault's Celebrated and Original Melodrama[2] (1897)

> Below is the last paragraph in a 64-page novella version, produced in a series announced as follows: "Into this Unique series of Stirring and Heart-Touching Tales, only those Powerful and Original Dramas are admitted which have achieved 'Undying Fame!'"

There is not much now to tell.

After the family had been reinstated in Terrebonne for some little time, Mrs. Peyton's Creole prejudices were overcome, and George married Zoe. The neighbours were somewhat scandalized at first; but when they saw that Dora Sunnyside, the wealthy heiress, stood by them thick and thin, they gradually came around. There are two little chubby babies, the offspring of the union—one is named Salem, and the other Dora. And it is whispered round about the Atchafalaya[3] that an older Salem and Dora are likely soon to make a match of it, following the example of George Peyton and his charming wife, ZOE, THE OCTOROON.

from Dion Boucicault, *The Octoroon*, Lacy's Acting Edition, No. 963 (c.1861)

> This four-act English version was published by T.H. Lacy, a London publisher. After the violent objections of English audiences to Zoe's suicide, Boucicault changed the ending to allow her to live. Many approving reviews written at the beginning of 1862 attest to the existence of this change, and include brief summaries of the new ending,

---

1 *denouemens* Denouement. The conclusion and final resolution of a plot.
2 *The Octoroon ... Original Melodrama* The series does not credit an author or editor.
3 *Atchafalaya* Area in southern Louisiana.

in which M'Closky flees with Zoe once his villainy is discovered; he is killed, not by Wahnotee, but by a bullet from George Peyton, which frees Zoe to leave America with Peyton. However, the acting edition (Lacy's Acting Edition), from which the following excerpt is taken, does not appear to follow the above plotline. Instead, this version entirely deletes Zoe's suicide scene, and moves from the dramatic climax of Act 3 (and the sale of Zoe in the auction) straight to the following scene, which constitutes the last act of the play. Although it does not confirm Zoe's death, it provides an ending that appears, at best, to be ambivalent, since Zoe's silent final appearance in George Peyton's arms does not necessarily mean she is alive.

ACT 4

(*The wharf.—The Steamer 'Magnolia' alongside, L.—A bluff rock, R.U.E.* RATTS *discovered, superintending the loading of ship. Enter* LAFOUCHE *and* JACKSON, *L.*)

JACKSON. How long before we start, captain?
RATTS. Just as soon as we put this cotton on board.

(*Enter* PETE, *with lantern, and* SCUDDER, *with notebook*, R.)

SCUDDER. One hundred and forty-nine bales. Can you take any more?
RATTS. Not a bale. I've got engaged eight hundred bales at the next landing, and one hundred hogsheads of sugar at Patten's Slide— that'll take my guards under—hurry up, thar!
VOICE. (*Outside.*) Wood's aboard.
RATTS. All aboard then.

(*Enter* M'CLOSKY, R.)

SCUDDER. Sign that receipt, captain, and save me going up to the clerk.
M'CLOSKY. See here—there's a small freight of turpentine in the forehold there, and one of the barrels leaks; a spark from your engines might set the ship on fire, and you'd go with it.
RATTS. You be darned! Go and try it if you've a mind to.
LAFOUCHE. Captain, you've loaded up here until the boat is sunk so deep in the mud she won't float.

RATTS. (*Calls off.*) Wood up thar, you Pollo—hang on to the safety valve—guess she'll crawl off on her paddles. (*Shouts heard*, R.)

JACKSON. What's the matter?

(*Enter* SOLON, R.)

SOLON. We got him!

SCUDDER. Who?

SOLON. The Inginn!

SCUDDER. Wahnotee? where is he? D'ye call running away from a fellow catching him?

RATTS. Here he comes.

OMNES. Where? where?

(*Enter* WAHNOTEE, R., *they are all about to rush on him.*)

SCUDDER. Hold on! Stan' round thar! No violence—the critter don't know what we mean.

JACKSON. Let him answer for the boy then.

M'CLOSKY. Down with him—lynch him.

OMNES. Lynch him!

(*Exit* LAFOUCHE, R.)

SCUDDER. Stan' back, I say! I'll nip the first that lays a finger on him. Pete, speak to the redskin.

PETE. Whar's Paul, Wahnotee? What's come ob de child?

WAHNOTEE. Paul wunce—Paul pangeuk.

PETE. Pangeuk—dead.

WAHNOTEE. Mort!

M'CLOSKY. And you killed him? (*They approach again.*)

SCUDDER. Hold on!

PETE. Um, Paul reste?

WAHNOTEE. Hugh vieu—(*Goes* L.)—Paul reste ci!

SCUDDER. Here, stay! (*Examines the ground.*) The earth has been stirred here lately.

WAHNOTEE. Weenee Paul. (*Points down and shows by pantomime how he buried* PAUL.)

SCUDDER. The Inginn means that he buried him there! Stop! Here's a bit of leather. (*Draws out mail-bags.*) The mail-bags that were lost! (*Sees tomahawk in* WAHNOTEE's *belt—draws it out and examines it.*) Look! Here are marks of blood—look that, red-skin, what's that?

WAHNOTEE. Paul! (*Makes sign that* PAUL *was killed by a blow on the head.*)

M'CLOSKY. He confesses it; the Indian got drunk, quarrelled with him, and killed him.

(*Re-enter* LAFOUCHE, R., *with smashed apparatus.*)

LAFOUCHE. Here are evidences of the crime; this rum bottle half emptied—this photographic apparatus smashed—and there are marks of blood and footsteps around the shed.

M'CLOSKY. What more d'ye want—ain't that proof enough? Lynch him!

OMNES. Lynch him! Lynch him!

SCUDDER. Stan' back, boys! he's an Inginn—fair play.

JACKSON. Try him, then—try him on the spot of his crime.

OMNES. Try him! try him!

LAFOUCHE. Don't let him escape!

RATTS. I'll see to that. (*Draws revolver.*) If he stirs, I'll put a bullet through his skull, might quick!

M'CLOSKY. Come—form a court, then, choose a jury—we'll fix this varmin.

(*Enter* THIBODEAUX *and* CAILLOU, L.)

THIBODEAUX. What's the matter?

LAFOUCHE. We've caught this murdering Inginn, and are going to try him.

(WAHNOTEE *sits* L., *rolled in blanket.*)

PETE. Poor little Paul—poor little nigger!

SCUDDER. This business goes agin me, Ratts—'taint right.

LAFOUCHE. We're ready, the jury is empanelled—go ahead—who'll be accuser?

RATTS. M'Closky.

M'CLOSKY. Me!

RATTS. Yes; you was the first to hail Judge Lynch.

M'CLOSKY (R.). Well, what's the use of argument, what guilt sticks out so plain; the boy and Inginn were alone when last seen.

SCUDDER (L.C.). Who says that?

M'CLOSKY. Everybody—that is, I heard so.

SCUDDER. Say what you know—not what you heard.

M'CLOSKY. I know then, that the boy was killed with that tomahawk—the redskin owns it—the signs of violence are all round the shed—this apparatus smashed—ain't it plain that in a drunken fit he slew the boy, and when sober concealed the body yonder?

OMNES. That's it—that's it.

RATTS. Who defends the Indian?

SCUDDER. I will; for it's agin my natur' to b'lieve him guilty; and if he be, this ain't the place, nor you the authority, to try him. How are we sure the boy is dead at all? There are no witnesses but a rum bottle and an old machine. Is it on such evidence you'd hang a human being?

RATTS. His own confession.

SCUDDER. I appeal against your usurped authority; this lynch law is a wild and lawless proceeding. Here's a picture for a civilised community to afford; yonder, a poor ignorant savage, and round him a circle of hearts, white with revenge and hate, thirsting for his blood; you call yourselves judges—you ain't—you're a jury of executioners. It is such scenes as these that bring disgrace on our Western life.

M'CLOSKY. Evidence! Evidence! Give us evidence, we've had talk enough; now for proof.

OMNES. Yes, yes! Proof, proof!

SCUDDER. Where am I to get it? The proof is here, in my heart!

PETE. (*Who has been looking about the camera.*) 'Top sar! 'Top a bit! Oh, laws-a-mussey, see dis, here's a pictur' I found sticking in that yar telescope machine, sar! Look, sar!

SCUDDER. A photographic plate. (PETE *holds the lantern up.*) What's this, eh? Two forms! The child—'tis he! Dead—and above him—Ah, ah! Jacob M'Closky—'twas you murdered that boy!

M'CLOSKY. Me?

SCUDDER. You! You slew him with that tomahawk, and as you stood over his body with the letter in your hand, you thought that no witness saw the deed, that no eye was on you; but there was, Jacob M'Closky, there was—the eye of the Eternal was on you—the blessed sun in heaven, that, looking down, struck upon this plate the image of the deed. Here you are, in the very attitude of your crime!

M'CLOSKY. 'Tis false!

SCUDDER. 'Tis true! The apparatus can't lie. Look there, jurymen—(*Shows plate to jury.*)—look there. Oh, you wanted evidence—you called for proof—heaven has answered and convicted you.

M'CLOSKY. What court of law would receive such evidence? (*Going.*)

RATTS. Stop, *this* would—you called it yourself; you wanted to make us murder that Inginn, and since we've got our hands in for justice, we'll try it on you. What say ye? Shall we have one law for the redskin and another for the white?

OMNES. Try him! Try him!

RATTS. Who'll be accuser.

SCUDDER. I will! Fellow citizens, you have convened and assembled here under a higher power than the law. What's the law? When the ship's abroad on the ocean—when the army is before the enemy—where in thunder's the law? It is in the hearts of brave men who can tell right from wrong, and from whom justice can't be bought. So it is here, in the Wilds of the West, where our hatred of crime is measured by the speed of our executions—where necessity is law!—I say, then, air you honest men? Air you true? Put your hands on your naked breasts, and let every man as don't feel a real American heart there, bustin' up with freedom, truth and right, let that man step out—that's the oath I put to ye—and then say, darn ye, go it!

OMNES. Go on—go on.

SCUDDER. No! I won't go on, that man's down, I won't strike him even with words. Jacob, your accuser is that picter of the crime—let that speak—defend yourself.

M'CLOSKY. (*Draws knife.*) I will, quicker than lightning.

RATTS. Seize him, then! (*They rush on* M'CLOSKY *and disarm him.*) He can fight, though—he's a painter, claws all over.

SCUDDER. Stop! Search him, we may find more evidence.

M'CLOSKY. Would you rob me first, and murder me afterwards?

RATTS. (*Searching him.*) That's his programme—here's a pocket-book.

SCUDDER. (*Opens it.*) What's here? Letters! hello! to "Mrs. Peyton, Terrebonne, Louisiana, United States" Liverpool post mark. Ho! I've got hold of the tail of a rat—come out. (*Reads.*) What's this?—a draft for 85,000 dollars and credit on Palisse and Co., of New Orleans, for the balance. Hi! the rat's out—you killed the boy to steal this letter from the mail-bags—you stole this letter that the money should not arrive in time to save the Octoroon; had it done so, the lien on the estate would have ceased, and Zoe would be free.

OMNES. Lynch him!—lynch him!—down with him!

SCUDDER. Silence in the court—stand back, let the gentlemen of the jury retire, consult, and return their verdict.

RATTS. I'm responsible for the crittur—go on.

PETE. (*To* WAHNOTEE.) See Inginn, look dar. (*Shows him plate.*) See dat innocent, look, dare's the murderer of poor Paul.

WAHNOTEE. Ugh! (*Examines plate.*)

PETE. Ya! as he? Closky tue Paul—kill de child with your tomahawk dar, 'twasn't you, no—ole Pete allus say so. Poor Inginn lub our little Paul.

(WAHNOTEE *rises and looks at* M'CLOSKY—*he is in his war paint and fully armed.*)

SCUDDER. What say ye, gentlemen? Is the prisoner guilty, or is he not guilty?

OMNES. Guilty!

SCUDDER. And what is to be his punishment?

OMNES. Death!

WAHNOTEE. (*Crosses to* M'CLOSKY.) Ugh!

SCUDDER. The Inginn, by thunder!

PETE. (*To* M'CLOSKY.) You's a dead man, mas'r; you've got to b'lieve dat.

M'CLOSKY. No! If I must die, give me up to the laws, but save me from the tomahawk of the savage; you are a white man, you'll not leave one of your own blood to be butchered by the scalping knife of the redskin.

SCUDDER. Hold on, now, Jacob, we've got to figure that out; let us look straight at the thing. Here we are on the confines of civilisation, it ain't our sile, I believe, rightly; Natur' has said that where the white man sets his foot the red man and the black man shall up sticks and stan' round. Now, what do we pay for that possession? In cash? No—in kind—that is, in protection and forbearance, in gentleness, and in all them goods that show the critters the difference between the Christian and the Savage. Now what you have done to show 'em the distinction? For darn me if I can find out.

M'CLOSKY. For what I've done let me be tried.

SCUDDER. Oh, you have been fairly and honestly tried, and convicted: Providence has chosen our executioner—I shan't interfere.

PETE. Oh! sar! hi, Mas'r Scudder, don't leave Mas'r M'Closky like dat—don't, sar—tain't what a good Christian would do.

SCUDDER. D'ye hear that, Jacob?—this old nigger, the grandfather of the boy you murdered, speaks for you—don't that go through ye—d'ye feel it? Go on, Pete, you've woke up the Christian here, and the old hoss responds.

WAHNOTEE. (*Placing his hand on* M'CLOSKY'*s head.*) Wahnotee!

SCUDDER. No, Inginn, we deal justice here, not revenge! 'tain't you he has injured, 'tis the white man, whose laws he has offended.

RATTS. Away with him! Put him down the hatch till we rig his funeral.

M'CLOSKY. Fifty against one! Oh! If you were alone—if I had ye one by one in the swamp, I'd rip ye all.

PETE. (*Lighting him off,* R.) Dis way, Mas'r 'Closky, take care, sar.

(*Exit with* M'CLOSKY *and* JACKSON *to steamer.*)

LAFOUCHE. Off with him, quick—here come the ladies.

(*Enter* MRS. CLAIBORNE, R I E.)

MRS. CLAIBORNE. Shall we soon start, Captain?

RATTS. Yes, ma'am; we've only got a—Take my hand, ma'am, to steady you—a little account to square, and we're off.

MRS. CLAIBORNE. A fog is rising.

RATTS. Swamp mist; soon clear off. (*Hands her to steamer.*)

MRS. CLAIBORNE. Good night.

RATTS. Good night, ma'am—good night.

SCUDDER. Now to business.

(PETE *appears on deck.*)

PETE. Oh! law, sar. Dat debbel, 'Closky—he tore hisself from de gentleman—knock me down—take away my light, and throwed it on de turpentine barrels—de ship's on fire!

(*All hurry off to ship—alarm bell rings—loud shouts; a hatch in the deck is opened—a glare of red—and* M'CLOSKY *emerges from the aperture; he is without his coat, and carries a bowie knife; he rushes down—*WAHNOTEE *alone is watching him from* R.U.E.)

M'CLOSKY. Ha, ha, ha! I've given them something to remember how they treated Jacob M'Closky. Made my way from one end of the vessel to the other, and now the road to escape is clear before me—and thus to secure it! (*He goes to* R.C., *and is met by* WAHNOTEE, *who silently confronts him.*)

WAHNOTEE. Paul.

M'CLOSKY. Devils!—you here!—stand clear!

WAHNOTEE. Paul.

M'CLOSKY. You won't!—die, fool!

(*Thrusts at him—*WAHNOTEE, *with his tomahawk, strikes the knife out of his hand;* M'CLOSKY *starts back;* WAHNOTEE *throws off his blanket, and strikes at* M'CLOSKY *several times, who avoids him; at last he catches his arm, and struggles for the tomahawk, which falls; a violent struggle and fight takes place, ending with the triumph of* WAHNOTEE, *who drags* M'CLOSKY *along the ground, takes up the knife and stabs him repeatedly;* GEORGE *enters, bearing* ZOE *in his arms—all the* CHARACTERS *rush on—noise increasing—The steam vessel blows up—grand Tableau, and*

CURTAIN

from Dion Boucicault, *The Octoroon: A Drama in Three Acts*[1] (26 October 1861)

In this version, the slave auction takes place at the end of Act 2. The original version is handwritten with no italics or other font changes. The spacing, spelling, capitalization, punctuation, etc. below have been edited to fit the original as much as possible.

---

1 *The Octoroon ... Three Acts* Licenser's Copy, Lord Chamberlain's Office. British Library collection. AD MS53008I

(*The outhouse in Terrebonne. Enter* MCCLOSKY *he looks around.*)

MCCLOSKY. Ah. This will do. (*Calls at door.*) Here—come in here. (*Enter* ZOE.) There—while they are selling off the livestock let us have a pow wow—you and me—so—I've got ye after all, Zoe— ain't I?

ZOE. Your [sic] are my slave say—

ZOE. [sic]: yes

MCCLOSKY. Yes, and a pooty tall price you ...[1] stood me in didn't ye—but I was bound to have ye if I sold my skin to foot the bill. And when they all got on me—must now they got the hair up on my back—I fell all over claw, and dangerous mad, that's a fact— but its gone now—so don't be skeered—I woudn't hurt ye—

ZOE. Hurt me—no—I cost too much.

MCCLOSKY. That's onkind—come, gal, praps I aint as bad as you reckon.

...[2]

What now if I ... gave you your freedom?

ZOE. I should nah believe you ... You mean to be kind, sir, but you are more cruel in your kindness ...

MCCLOSKY. Cruel! What when I offer to make you my wife!

ZOE. I'd rather be your slave!

MCCLOSKY. The Hell you would—do you know that you are mine, full mine—anyway I know it.

...[3]

Tableau—Stage becomes dark—The scene above opens and discovers the scene of the Landing ... RH—the River at the back— the body of McClosky is lying across the ... his face and neck traversed with blood—the Indian Wahnotee is passing p—the ...

---

1   ...   The handwritten text in the original is illegible here.

2   ...   A large section is crossed out here. Some words can be made out, however, and indicate this was an extended section in which he justifies his bitterness towards everyone: "It's the talk around here that ... folks around here have cut me ... abused me ... like a rat in a hole."

3   ...   Zoe leaves soon after this, and the scene moves towards the ending where McClosky is discovered to be the villain, and more or less the confrontation with accusers and Scudder, and the same speeches by Scudder about justice are used. The play ends with the tableau— much is cut out in the manuscript or left unwritten.

On Slavery

from Dion Boucicault, unpublished note, Theatre Museum, London (1861)

The word Octoroon signifies "one-eighth blood" or the child of a Quadroon by a white. The Octoroons have no apparent trace of the negro in their appearance but still are subject to the legal disabilities which attach them to the condition of blacks. The plot of this drama was suggested to the author by the following incident, which occurred in Louisiana and came under his notice during his residence in that state. The laws of Louisiana forbid the marriage of a white man with any woman having the smallest trace of black blood in her veins. The Quadroon and Octoroon girls, proud of their white blood, revolt from union with the blacks and are unable to form marriages with the white. They are thus driven into an equivocal position and form a section of New Orleans society, resembling the demi-monde[1] of Paris. A young and wealthy planter of Louisiana fell deeply and sincerely in love with a Quadroon girl of great beauty and purity. The lovers found their union opposed by the law; but love knows no obstacles. The young man, in the presence of two friends, who served as witnesses, opened a vein in his arms and introduced into it a few drops of his mistress's blood; thus he was able to make oath that he had black blood in his veins, and being attested the marriage was performed. The great interest now so broadly felt in American affairs induces the author to present "The Octoroon" as the only American drama which has hitherto attempted to portray American homes, American scenery, and manners without either exaggeration or prejudice. The author has been informed of the strong objection to the scenes in this drama representing the slave sale at which Zoe is sold and to avoid her fate commits suicide. It has been stated that such circumstances are wholly improbable. In reply to these remarks he begs to quote from Slave history the following episode: a young lady named Miss Winchester, the daughter of a wealthy planter in Kent had been educated in Boston where she was received in the best

---

1 *demi-monde* French: shadowy world (literally, half world); euphemism for a world of loose morality and prostitution.

circles of society and universally admired for her great beauty and accomplishments. The news of her father's sudden death recalled her to Kentucky. Examination into the affairs of the deceased revealed the fact that Miss Winchester was the natural child of the planter by a quadroon slave; she was inventoried in chattels of the estate, and sold; the next day her body was found floating in the Ohio.

from Fredrika Bremer,[1] "Fredrika Bremer Sees the New Orleans Slave Market" (1853)

The great slave-market is held in several houses situated in a particular part of the city. One is soon aware of their neighborhood from the groups of colored men and women, of all shades between black and light yellow, which stand or sit unemployed at the doors. ...

Among the women, who were few in number in comparison with the men (there might be from seventy to eighty of them), there were some very pretty light mulattos. A gentleman took one of the prettiest by the chin, and opened her mouth to see the state of her gums and teeth, with no more ceremony than if she had been a horse. Had I been in her place, I believe I should have bitten his thumb, so much did I feel myself irritated by his behavior, in which he evidently, no more than she, found any thing offensive. Such is the custom of the place. ...

On the 31st of December I went ... to witness a slave-auction ... It was held at one of the small auction-rooms which are found in various parts of New Orleans. The principal scene of slave-auctions is a splendid rotunda,[2] the magnificent dome of which is worthy to resound with songs of freedom. ...

... I entered a large and somewhat cold and dirty hall, on the basement story of a house, and where a great number of people were assembled. About twenty gentlemanlike men stood in a half circle around a dirty wooden platform, which for the moment was unoccupied. On each side, by the wall, stood a number of black men and women, silent and serious. The whole assembly was silent, and it seemed to me as if a heavy gray cloud rested upon it.

---

1 *Fredrika Bremer* A visitor from Sweden, Fredrika Bremer witnessed a slave market in New Orleans in December 1840.
2 *rotunda* Circular building often with a domed roof.

[The auctioneer, an Englishman, now enters] He took the auctioneer's hammer in his hand, and addressed the assembly much as follows:

"The slaves which I have now to sell, for what price I can get, are a few home-slaves, all the property of one master. This gentleman having given his bond for a friend who afterward became bankrupt, has been obliged to meet his responsibilities by parting with his faithful servants. These slaves are thus sold, not in consequence of any faults which they possess, or for any deficiencies. They are all faithful and excellent servants, and nothing but hard necessity would have compelled their master to part with them. They are worth the highest price, and he who purchases them may be sure that he increases the prosperity of his family."

After this he beckoned to a woman among the blacks to come forward, and he gave her his hand to mount upon the platform, where she remained standing beside him. She was a tall, well-grown mulatto, with a handsome but sorrowful countenance, and a remarkably modest, noble demeanor. She bore on her arm a young sleeping child, upon which, during the whole auction ceremonial, she kept her eyes immovably riveted, with her head cast down. She wore a gray dress made to the throat, and a pale yellow handkerchief, checked with brown, was tied round her head.

The auctioneer now began to laud the woman's good qualities, her skill, and her abilities, to the assembly. He praised her character, her good disposition, order, fidelity; her uncommon qualifications for taking care of a house; her piety, her talents, and remarked that the child which she bore at her breast, and which was to be sold with her, also increased her value. After this he shouted with a loud voice, "Now, gentlemen, how much for this very superior woman, this remarkable, &c., &c., and her child?"

He pointed with his outstretched arm and fore-finger from one to another of the gentlemen who stood around, and first one and then another replied to his appeal with a sort silent nod, and all the while he continued in this style:

"Do you offer me five hundred dollars? Gentlemen, I am offered five hundred dollars for this superior woman and her child. It is a sum not to be thought of! She, with her child, is worth double that money. Five hundred and fifty, six hundred, six hundred and fifty, six hundred and sixty, six hundred and seventy. My good gentlemen, why do you not at once say seven hundred dollars for this uncommonly superior woman and her child? Seven hundred dollars—it is downright robbery! She would never have been sold at that price if her master had not been so unfortunate," &c., &c.

The hammer fell heavily; the woman and her child were sold for seven hundred dollars to one of those dark, silent figures before her. Who he was; whether he was good or bad; whether he would lead her into tolerable or intolerable slavery—of all this, the bought and sold woman and mother knew as little as I did. ...

After this came an elderly woman, who had also one of those good-natured, excellent countenances so common among the black population, and whose demeanor and general appearance showed that she too had been in the service of a good master, and, having been accustomed to gentle treatment, had become gentle and happy. All these slaves ... bore the impression of having been accustomed to an affectionate family life.

And now, what was to be their future fate? How bitterly, if they fell into the hands of the wicked, would they feel the difference between then and now—how horrible would be their lot! ...

No sermon, no anti-slavery oration could speak so powerfully against the institution of slavery as this slave-auction itself!

The master had been good, the servants good also, attached, and faithful, and yet they were sold to whoever would buy them—sold like brute beasts!

from *Civil Code of the State of Louisiana* (1825)

The following articles formed part of the Louisiana legal framework governing slavery. Note the codes about inheritance of the state of slavery through the mother, and about the connection between outstanding debts and mortgages and a slave owner's ability to free a slave.

ART. 182.—Slaves cannot marry without the consent of their masters, and their marriages do not produce any of the civil effects which result from such contract.

ART. 183.—Children born of a mother then in a state of slavery, whether married or not, follow the condition of their mother; they are consequently slaves and belong to the master of their mother.

ART. 184.—A master may manumit[1] his slave in this State, either by an act *inter vivos*[2] or by a disposition made in prospect of death, provided such manumission[3] be made with the forms and under the conditions prescribed by law; but an enfranchisement, when made by a last will, must be express and formal, and shall not be implied by any other circumstances of the testament, such as a legacy, and institution of heir, testamentary executorship or other dispositions of this nature, which, in such case, shall be considered as if they had not been made.

ART. 185.—No one can emancipate his slave, unless the slave has attained the age of thirty years, and has behaved well for at least four years preceding his emancipation.

ART. 187.—The master who wishes to emancipate his slave, is bound to make a declaration of his intentions to the judge of the parish where he resides; the judge must order notice of it to be published during forty days by advertisement posted at the door of the court

---

1   *manumit*   To set free a slave.
2   *inter vivos*   Latin: between the living. This legal term implies that a gift or transfer is made during an individual's lifetime rather than through a testamentary transfer (or will) upon their death.
3   *manumission*   Act of freeing one's slave.

house; and if, at the expiration of this delay, no opposition be made, he shall authorise the master to pass the act of emancipation.

ART. 190.—Any enfranchisement made in fraud of creditors, or of the portion reserved by law to forced heirs is null and void; and such fraud shall be considered as proved, when it shall appear that at the moment of executing the enfranchisement, the person granted it had not sufficient property to pay his debts or to leave to his heirs the portion to them reserved by law; the same rule will apply if the slave thus manumitted, was specially mortgaged; but in this case the enfranchisement shall take effect, provided the slave or any one on his behalf shall pay the debt for which the mortgage was given.

Illustrations

from *The Illustrated London News* (30 November 1861)

The following text accompanied the illustration reproduced on the cover of this book, the caption for which was "Scene from Mr. Boucicault's New Drama. The Slave Market—Sale of the Octoroon."

We have selected the "sensation scene" from Mr. Boucicault's new drama of "The Octoroon" for an illustration this week. This particular scene recommends itself from its truthfulness. In delineating the dreadful business which it represents, the dramatist has attempted no exaggeration. He has treated it as a familiar horror, one which society has accepted as portion of the regular business of the market and legalised as an institution. However abominable it may be, it is authorised. Those who observe, and those who are actively engaged in the transaction, alike acquiesce in the fact and the principle, as if there were no outrage being done to nature, no sin against humanity committed. Any external demonstration of excitement would be improper. What conflict there is goes on within. That beautiful Octoroon—what feels she? They who would save her from the threatened degradation—what feel they? And in that determined wretch, who exceeds his means in her purchase—O! What a hell there is in his bosom, of premeditated guilt, and even already of an anticipated remorse! The picture is presented on the stage in fine taste.

There can be no doubt that if it had been morally possible for the author to have given a happier ending to his drama it would have been more immediately popular. But we do not think that this circumstance will at all interfere with its run. The audience take all through a strong interest in the fate of the heroine, and this is manifested by the reluctance they feel at the end when the victim finds no refuge but in death.

REYNOLDS'S MISCELLANY

Of Romance, General Literature, Science, and Art.

No. 708. [Vol. XXVIII.]   SATURDAY, JANUARY 4, 1862.   [Price One Penny.

THE OCTOROON

WRITTEN EXPRESSLY FOR THIS JOURNAL, AND FOUNDED ON THE DRAMA OF THAT NAME, BY D. BOUCICAULT, ESQ.

Cover, *Reynolds Miscellany* (4 January 1862). This periodical found *The Octoroon* sensational enough to illustrate its cover with scenes from the play. The central auction scene is framed by other dramatic points, such as M'Closky's murder of Paul and discovery of the documents and several scenes of confrontation between Wahnotee and M'Closky.

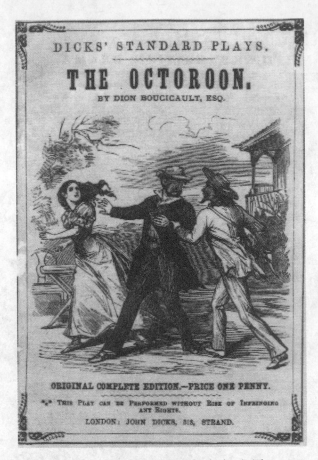

DICKS' STANDARD PLAYS.

THE OCTOROON.

BY DION BOUCICAULT, ESQ.

ORIGINAL COMPLETE EDITION.—PRICE ONE PENNY.

** THIS PLAY CAN BE PERFORMED WITHOUT RISK OF INFRINGING ANY RIGHTS.

LONDON: JOHN DICKS, 313, STRAND.

Cover, *The Octoroon* (Dick's Standard Plays). This cover
of a penny edition (Dick's Standard Plays) focuses on
Scudder's attempt to protect Zoe from M'Closky.

Permissions Acknowledgments

"Pan at the Play," from *Fun*, December 21, 1861: page 135. Retrieved from http://ufdc.ufl.edu/UF00078627/00001/140x?search=fun& vo=3. University of Florida, George A. Smathers Libraries.

Playbill for *The Octoroon* and *The Colleen Bawn*, from *Dion Boucicault: A Biography*, by Richard Fawkes. London: Quartet, 1979. Reprinted with the permission of the Boucicault Archive, Special Collections, University of Kent.

"Zoe the Octoroon Galop" [P.F. with cornet accompaniment], 1862. Charles Coote the Younger. h.2948.(20.) Copyright © the British Library Board.

from the publisher

A name never says it all, but the word "broadview" expresses a good deal of the philosophy behind our company. We are open to a broad range of academic approaches and political viewpoints. We pay attention to the broad impact book publishing and book printing has in the wider world; we began using recycled stock more than a decade ago, and for some years now we have used 100% recycled paper for most titles. As a Canadian-based company we naturally publish a number of titles with a Canadian emphasis, but our publishing program overall is internationally oriented and broad-ranging. Our individual titles often appeal to a broad readership too; many are of interest as much to general readers as to academics and students.

Founded in 1985, Broadview remains a fully independent company owned by its shareholders—not an imprint or subsidiary of a larger multinational.

If you would like to find out more about Broadview and about the books we publish, please visit us at **www.broadviewpress.com**. And if you'd like to place an order through the site, we'd like to show our appreciation by extending a special discount to you: by entering the code below you will receive a 20% discount on purchases made through the Broadview website.

Discount code: **broadview20%**

Thank you for choosing Broadview.

Please note: this offer applies only to sales of bound books within the United States or Canada.

The interior of this book is printed on 100% recycled paper.